TRANSFORM PRESSURE TO POWER

Helen Davis

ISBN: 9781097707836

To Kelly

Wishing you every success

Helen

CONTENTS

ABOUT THE AUTHOR

Helen is an experienced Rider Psychology Coach with a passion for helping riders transform their confidence and focus at competition and in everyday riding so they can achieve their goals. The people she coaches learn to:

✓ Overcome their fears and strengthen their self-belief.

✓ Ride to the best of their ability at home and at competition.

✓ Get to that sweet spot where competing feels easy and fun.

✓ Achieve the results they work so hard for.

Her approach to coaching riders has been shaped by her personal experience and awareness that your life can change in the blink of an eye and that you can lose the person that you were in a single moment. Several years ago, a serious riding accident left Helen with an injured neck and shattered nerves. While her body healed, the psychological trauma lingered. She lost her confidence, and with it, her joy for riding. She spent eighteen months identifying what was effective and what wasn't, resulting in the creation of her own framework and methodology for helping riders experiencing confidence and focus issues at all levels, from amateur to professional.

Helen believes that each rider has unique experiences and needs, which means that each of her coaching sessions are bespoke and tailored to the rider's personal challenges and aspirations.

The techniques that Helen uses, which you'll get insights in to throughout this book, comprise of sports psychology, Neuro-Linguistic Programming (NLP) and hypnosis techniques.

FOREWORD

Riding and training horses is nothing short of a privilege and a pleasure and I have had a career at a professional level that I could only have dreamed of and am completely humbled by, everyday.

Inevitably with horses, situations can present themselves that challenge our confidence. Nerves can quickly deteriorate our abilities, so it is essential that we have the tools to overcome these hurdles, many of which I believe you will find in this book.

The Olympic Games in Rio De Janeiro in 2016 was an experience I have never felt before in terms of my confidence. As Valegro and I were walking to the arena, I turned to Carl and told him I couldn't ride, that I couldn't feel my legs and in turn, couldn't do the test. He reassured me, I collected my thoughts and at that same moment, it felt as though Valegro took hold of my hand and said 'Mum, we can do this' At that split second and thanks to a horse who knows it's job, I had the strength and tools to know how to override my thoughts and deliver for my country and that it why rider psychology is so important to me.

The strategies herein will help you recognise those crippling signs and help you understand how you can manage these situations as they arise. Whether you are aiming for the championship level or simply wish to reconnect with your horse and your riding, Transform Pressure to Power by Helen Davis will shift your mindset, and enable you to overthrow your inner negativity, so you can reconnect with your horse and love of the sport.

It is a privilege to have been asked to write this foreword for Helen and I hope you enjoy this book and all that it offers, as much as I have.

– Charlotte Dujardin CBE

DEDICATION

This book is dedicated to you, the reader of this book because I understand how difficult it can be to overcome loss of confidence and focus. Knowing where to start, what action to take, what solutions will work best for you; it can feel overwhelming. Taking the first step is often the hardest.

That's why I've written this book to help you start on the journey of regaining your confidence and focus by helping you identify the root cause of the problems you're experiencing and the solutions that are most likely to work best for you.

This book is also dedicated to the equine. The beautifully elegant animal who asks us for very little and yet willingly gives us their trust, understanding and energy. Whose confidence often relies on the confidence of the rider, their leader. So this book is as much about improving the partnership with your horse as it is about your mindset.

In each chapter you'll find exercises to help you gain deeper insights in to your mindset and give you simple tools and techniques to help you start to build confidence and focus, whether you are hacking, schooling, training or competing, strategies in this book can help you.

This book has been designed to be read in a non-sequential way, which means you can start wherever you want, reading chapters one at a time. The chapters are not linked, deliberately, so that even if you have just 30 minutes a day, you can still gain value from the mindset strategies and exercises.

Think of each chapter as a coaching session on a particular subject so make sure you have some dedicated time to work through it. Remember that everyone is different, so adapt each exercise so that it is tailored to you. Wishing you every success!

ACKNOWLEDGEMENTS

Writing this book may have been a solitary exercise but it's been inspired by so many people. Firstly, a massive thank you to Charlotte Dujardin CBE, Triple Olympic Gold Medalist and a World Champion superstar for kindly contributing an empowering and inspiring foreword. There could not be a more fitting introduction to my book and I am genuinely touched that Charlotte took time out of her busy schedule to share her insights and experience.

Front cover photograph with kind permission of Paul Ruffle.

Thanks also to Abby Newell for inspiring me to write a second edition of this book and for her creative input, and to Natalie Heaton for designing and formatting the entire book cover-to- cover.

My heartfelt thank you to all the special people in my life - you know who you are - who have consistently believed in me, supported me and encouraged me even in the most difficult of times.

Thanks also to Peter Haynes, master coach and 1998 Australian International three day Eventing Champion, for inspiring me to rebuild my confidence after my riding accident and showed me that my dream job was somewhere outside the corporate world. It's been a wonderful journey.

Finally, this book is in memory of my amazing first horse Floyd, who was an incredible schoolmaster and a once in a lifetime horse. Although he is gone, he will never be forgotten.

NOTE TO READER

The information, including opinion and analysis, contained herein is based on the author's personal experiences and is not intended to provide professional advice.

The author and the publisher make no warranties, either expressed or implied, concerning the accuracy, applicability, effectiveness, reliability or suitability of the contents. If you wish to apply or follow the advice or recommendations mentioned herein, you take full responsibility for your actions. The author and publisher of this book shall in no event be held liable for any direct, indirect, incidental or consequential damages arising directly or indirectly from the use of any of the information contained in this book.

All content is for information only and is not warranted for content accuracy or any other implied or explicit purpose.

WHY MINDSET MATTERS
MY STORY

The most wonderful memory I have of riding is cantering through beautiful woodland. I remember it so vividly that if I close my eyes now, I can still feel the softness of the woodland surface beneath me, hear the hypnotic rhythm of hooves making contact with the ground, smell the wild garlic that surrounded us, feeling a sense of freedom and utter joy. Being completely in the moment.

It's ironic that this is my favourite memory of my time with my first horse Floyd. As an experienced dressage and showjumping horse, he taught me a lot and we were a competitive partnership. So it's funny that I don't remember the rosette winning moments with as much fondness.

Maybe it's because my focus at competitions was on judging how I was riding, concerning myself with whether I was riding well rather than simply being immersed in the moment. Maybe it's because there was something special about that woodland. You could only access it by crossing a river, something that Floyd was less than enthusiastic about. After all, there could be crocodiles lurking underneath the surface of all that water. So getting across the river was a challenge. I'd encourage him down the bank. He'd promptly then run backwards, which was quite a feat considering he was running backwards uphill.

Then I'd try again, and he'd run backwards again. We'd continue this strange moonwalking dance for a while until I managed to slowly encourage him to the edge of the water. Weirdly, once he was at the edge of the water, he'd stretch down to sniff it, then he'd step right in, splash around for a bit, playing with the water, then happily walk right across the river to the other side and up the bank to start a long canter through the beautiful woodland.

Confidence was rarely an issue with Floyd. I trusted him and he trusted me. We worked well as a partnership and he was my ideal first horse. I remember my first competition with him. I was pretty nervous, worrying about all sorts of things, but he remained calm and helped me focus. That's one of the things I loved most about him. He was no different at competition to how he was at home, even if I was nervous.

He had his quirks; running backwards was an evasion he used a lot, and if you asked him to jump a course more than twice a week he'd start putting in stops at fences. He could be opinionated but as long as you understood him and worked with him, he was your best friend.

It all changed when Floyd fractured his pelvis in the field. Whilst he managed 16 weeks of box rest with stoic resolve and the fracture healed, the trauma caused the onset of hip arthritis.

Hip arthritis is very difficult to treat and despite all my best efforts and excellent veterinary care, it was simply a matter of time before the lameness would become so severe he would have to be put to sleep.

The pain of losing Floyd was suffocating. I was inconsolable when the time came to say goodbye. It was one of the toughest decisions I've ever made but it came from a place of love and determination that he would not suffer. His wellbeing was more important to me than anything else. There are few things in this world that I will ever love as much as I loved Floyd.

After the devastation of losing Floyd, finding another horse was difficult. The main problem was that I was too emotional to make the right decision. So I made an unwise choice and bought a project horse that was simply too much of a challenge for me. I should have known better. Oz reared and unseated me when I went to try him. That should have been enough of a warning. But in my grief stricken state, I made a decision that would make me realise the importance of mindset.

About a month after I bought Oz, I was thrown off in the outdoor arena and lay unconscious for several minutes whilst an ambulance was called. One of the other liveries saw it happen and told me it looked like a triple somersault dismount and that I had landed on my neck. I didn't remember anything. But the trauma of what had happened left a lasting mark on my mindset.

Overnight my confidence was shattered. I didn't want to get back on and even when I eventually managed to find the courage to mount up, I struggled to do anything other than walk and a few strides of trot. My confidence had deserted me and taken my riding skills with it. I realised that unless I got help, I was going to struggle to continue to ride. Then I'd have not only lost Floyd, I'd have lost my love of riding.

The thought of not riding again was unbearable. So I decided to take a step into the unknown and invest in getting some help to regain my confidence. It was a tough decision. I still had livery to pay for and I had no guarantee that anything would work, but making that decision changed my life. It didn't just result in me regaining my confidence. It also gave me a passion for helping others, because I realised that many riders experience loss of confidence and focus, both in everyday riding and at competition.

It set me on a path of discovery and learning, gaining in depth insights in to the way we think and react when we are under pressure, when our confidence is tested. I learnt how we think affects the way we feel and how our emotions affect the way we react. I understood how different techniques and approaches in sports psychology and Neuro-Linguistic Programming (NLP) could be combined and used to help riders overcome anxiety, nerves and stress to build confidence and focus.

Working with psychology coaches at the peak of their career I learnt how techniques are applied across all sports at amateur, professional and elite levels which enabled me to adapt techniques to equestrian sport.

Helping riders to overcome mindset challenges they thought insurmountable and seeing the joy that it gives them to be liberated from the problems that were holding them back, able to ride and compete confidently, gives me almost as much joy as that memory of cantering through the woodland with Floyd. It is my passion and love of equestrian sport that drives me. Knowing that I can make a significant positive difference to not just the rider but the partnership they have with their horse through building the rider's confidence and focus, believing in them throughout the coaching process and supporting them to achieve goals they thought were out of reach.

So although this is my story, this is simply my way of enabling you to get to know me a little better. So you can come on a journey with me throughout this book as I guide you through a series of mindset strategies and techniques to help you overcome anxiety, stress and self-doubt, so you can ride more confidently with more focus, whether your goal is to enjoy everyday riding or achieve a specific competition outcome.

THE PRESSURE PROBLEM

Pressure is a more common problem amongst riders than you may think. It can be difficult to tell if a rider is dealing with pressure effectively or whether it is affecting how they think, feel and ride. If you look closely enough though, you can see the negative effects of pressure in many everyday riding and competition situations.

Riders freeze, ride defensively, become a passenger, hold their breath, get visibly stressed and make mistakes. These are all symptoms of stress, anxiety and nerves, caused by pressure.

Many riders think that pressure is caused by the situation they are in and that they have no ability to change it; little do they realise that they can control the effect that pressure has on the way they think, feel and ride.

Pressure exists almost everywhere in our daily lives; it is unavoidable, but it isn't always negative. Whether you experience the negative effects of pressure when you ride at home, out hacking or at competition, recognising and dealing with the source of pressure is key to helping you enjoy and gain a sense of achievement from your riding.

How you respond to pressure is determined by whether you perceive pressure as a positive influence or a problem. Some riders use pressure to help them focus on the task in hand and ride to the best of their ability; they see pressure as a positive challenge, something that enables them to achieve their goals.

When they are under pressure, they maintain their confidence and focus. Other riders see pressure as oppressive, something that limits them, making them feel anxious and nervous which results in a loss of confidence or focus. Rather than an enabler, pressure is seen as a blocker to achieving goals.

This difference isn't about natural talent and it isn't about level of riding skill. It is about mindset and your skill in controlling your thoughts and feelings. It's about how you think and act under pressure, which means your thoughts and actions will either allow you to simply survive or enable you to thrive under pressure.

Before we explore the mindset strategies, it is important to identify the sources of pressure that cause loss of confidence and focus. These vary from rider to rider so understanding what creates negative pressure for you is a key first step to changing how you think, feel and react. In my experience as a Rider Psychology Coach, the most common sources of pressures for riders are:

- Worrying about 'what if' scenarios

- Fear of losing control

- Negative focus, i.e. focusing on the negatives of a situation and not acknowledging the positives

- Focusing on perfection

- Setting high expectations, which can be self-imposed or created through pressure of other people's expectations of you and/or your horse

- Striving to achieve specific outcome, e.g. qualification for a championship, specific dressage score, team selection

- Self-doubt. This can take many forms including: being overly critical of yourself, worrying about what other people think, worrying about doing your horse justice, feeling that you're not good enough, doubting your ability, not trusting your judgement and overthinking.

CREATING CONFIDENCE AND FOCUS

You may be wondering how it is possible to transform your mindset from anxiety and stress to confidence and focus. Often a challenging part of changing your mindset is the belief that you can think and feel differently because you can get stuck in a negative loop of thinking negatively, feeling anxious and nervous and not achieving your goals.

The idea that you could become more confident and focused, and achieve your goals, can seem like a distant dream. The key to overcoming this is to first recognise the problems you're experiencing so that you can identify the correct solutions.

Taking this first step requires courage to reflect on what you're thinking and feeling. It's normal for this to feel like a difficult step, so I urge you to be kind to yourself, take time and recognise that you can only become more resilient to pressure if you face and overcome the challenges you're experiencing. Remember that you don't have to do this alone. Having positive support around you will help you throughout this process.

This book is designed to help you overcome the negative effects of pressure and create more positive riding experiences, in everyday riding, training and competing, so you can achieve your goals.

It doesn't matter whether you ride for fun, compete as an amateur or ride professionally, the mindset strategies in this book are suitable for riders across all levels and can be used in any riding situation where you experience anxiety, nerves, stress or self-doubt.

The key to overcoming problems created by pressure is to change how you react. Your reactions are determined by how you think, which is why this book focuses on ways to change your thinking in small, manageable and sustainable steps.

It's not about simply flicking a switch to think positively. It's about practical and achievable steps to changing the way you think, which will change the way you react and ride under pressure. That's why I've designed this book to be read non-sequentially, which means you get to choose where you start and where you finish.

You can choose to read the book cover to cover or, if like many riders, you don't have a lot of time and simply want to read about the strategies that are most relevant to you, then you can focus on specific chapters.

You may notice that this book contains a number of specific mindset strategies rather than a series of general principles.

That is because I believe the process of building confidence, focus and mental resilience is not as simple as thinking positively or 'faking it until you make it.' These are very general, 'global' strategies that do not directly address the source of a pressure problem.

Each chapter is like a coaching session, with tools, techniques and actions to help you change your mindset. So it doesn't matter if it takes you a few weeks or several months to read this book; simply go at the pace that works best for you.

In each chapter you'll discover different techniques that will help you improve your confidence and mental resilience. The techniques that will be most helpful to you will depend on the problems you're experiencing at the moment. Later in this chapter, you'll find a short, simple questionnaire to help you identify the techniques that will work best for you.

The techniques in this book focus on different aspects of a rider's mindset and are organized in to, eight mindset strategies:

1. Self-Belief: how to improve your self belief, by increasing the power of positive beliefs and challenging negative beliefs.

2. Performance Profiling: how to use a simple framework to improve your positive focus.

3. Mental Rehearsal: how to use visualization to overcome stressful situations and ride more positively.

4. Dealing with your inner critic: how to stop being tough on yourself and be more positive.

5. Master your emotions: how to remain in control of your emotions in difficult situations.

6. Develop positive focus: how to avoid distractions and remain positively focused when you ride and compete.

7. Rituals and routines: gain confidence by using rituals and routines that help you remain calm and in control.

8. Triggers: how to establish triggers for confidence that you can use whenever you feel anxious, nervous or stressed.

MINDSET SUCCESS FACTORS

Now that you know a little more about the mindset strategies in this book, you may be wondering what it takes to create a confident and resilient rider mindset. Underpinning each of the mindset strategies and techniques in this book, are seven critical success factors. Each of these factors is an important building block for confidence, focus and resilience.

So let's examine each one so you understand the fundamental success factors and can identify your areas of strength, as well as identify opportunities for improvement.

1. The 4 Cs – Confidence, Commitment, Control and Challenge. You need each of these elements to be well balanced to develop a confident and resilient mindset. Fine-tuning these elements to suit your level of skill and goals is critical to helping you consistently ride to the best of your ability.

2. Self-belief – this is the foundation upon which your confidence and ability to ride positively under pressure is built. Belief shapes achievement and achievement shapes belief! Unless you overcome negative, limiting beliefs, you won't be able to consistently ride at your best, especially when you are under pressure. I've

dedicated a full chapter in this book to belief, because it's so fundamental to your ability to ride at your best and achieve your goals. Once you build greater self-belief, your perspective on your riding performance will change for the better and you'll gain the momentum and confidence you need to consistently ride at your best.

3. Motivation – feeling motivated to achieve something that genuinely excites you is incredibly important for confidence and focus. If you don't feel motivated, if you feel like you 'should' achieve a particular goal, it is likely that you won't take the actions required to improve your skills and mindset, so your riding performance won't improve. You will only ride at your best if you feel motivated to do so.

4. Focus – riding is a high mental skill sport so you need to be able to concentrate over a long period and make quick decisions at speed. There are so many external variables when you ride and compete, it's easy to get overwhelmed or focus on the things you cannot control. When you do this, you'll find it difficult to ride at your best. When you fine-tune your mindset, you'll find it easier to focus on the things you can control, which will enable you to ride more consistently at your best.

5. Mental Toughness – your ability to overcome setbacks and adversity is critical. Being able to deal with the highs and lows of riding and competing is one of the keys to riding to the best of your ability. The path to success is filled with obstacles, so the fact that you encounter and overcome setbacks means you're on the right track!

6. Performance zone – to consistently ride at your best, it's important to be in your performance zone when you're riding and competing. You're in your performance zone when you're motivated, focused on the task of riding and able to make quick decisions. When you're in your zone,

you're completely immersed in the present moment, everything flows and you're able to zero in on the task in hand. You may not be aware of it, but when you perform at your best, you are in your performance zone.

7. Switching off autopilot – to improve your mindset, it's important to identify your negative mental habits: what you tend to think and feel and how that affects your riding. Once you've gained these insights, then you must be willing to invest energy in switching off autopilot! We operate on autopilot most of the time because we have deeply ingrained habits, some of which prevent us from riding at our best. Being able to overcome negative mental habits is key to improving confidence, self-belief and focus. Our brains are programmed to operate out of habit irrespective of whether our habits are good or bad. Most of the time we're unaware of our habits. However, you have a choice about whether to simply keep doing things on autopilot or whether to break the pattern and build a new, more helpful habit that will help you to ride at your best. When you start to make changes to your mindset and you start to break one or more habits, it will be difficult initially because you have to re-program your brain. However, the great thing about our brains is that they are extremely flexible and there is overwhelming evidence that we can learn new habits at any stage in our life. This means that once you start to switch off autopilot and apply new mindset strategies consistently, you'll be able to build a brand new habit that will enable you to perform at your best and unlock your full riding potential. Persistence is key.

ACTION

Throughout this book you'll find Action sections. These sections are designed to focus you on key steps to help you improve your confidence and focus. I invite you to think of each of these actions as opportunities to improve your mindset and be curious about how each of the action steps can help you. If you find some actions work better than others, that's OK. It's perfectly normal because everyone is different. So take the actions and measure the results without judgement. Simply observe and note the actions that give you the best results.

With that in mind, I'd like you to reflect on your rider mindset and identify your top three habits that stop you riding at your best under pressure, whether it's in everyday riding that you experience pressure or at competition. Review your past riding experiences to identify where each habit originated from; it could be a specific experience or a series of experiences that caused the habit to develop and become well established. Then consider the three new habits you'd like to establish instead that would help you to ride at your best. Keep it simple because it's simple changes that are the key to building new habits for peak performance. Keep a note of these new habits you'd like to create as you work through each chapter because the mindset strategies you need to start making the changes you want are right here in this book.

GETTING STARTED

Often the hardest part of working on your mindset is getting started. So it's important that you start with focusing on a mindset strategy that is directly relevant to the problems you are currently experiencing so you can make positive progress more quickly, which will give you momentum to keep going. I believe that 'one size fits all' is a fundamentally flawed approach for making significant and long lasting changes to your mindset. My philosophy is different. I believe that every rider is unique and that all the mindset strategies and techniques from sports psychology and NeuroLinguistic Programming (NLP), can only be valuable and effective if they are tailored to the rider. That means that the starting point for working on your mindset is you.

So to help you get started, I've designed a simple questionnaire that will identify the mindset strategies that are most relevant to you. The higher the score, the more important the mindset strategy will be in helping you to improve your confidence and focus under pressure. This will help you prioritise the mindset strategies and you can then read the chapters in that exact sequence. Some riders find that two or three mindset strategies are relevant to them, whereas others find that most of the mindset strategies are relevant and it is simply a question of prioritising them according to score. You can of course decide to read this book sequentially, moving from chapter to chapter until you reach the end. Just do whatever you feel will work best for you.

RIDER MINDSET STRATEGY QUESTIONNAIRE

This questionnaire is designed to highlight the mindset strategies that are most relevant to you and direct you to the appropriate chapters in the book.

First, think about recent riding experiences (e.g. competition, lesson, schooling, hacking) where you felt under pressure and experienced anxiety, nerves or stress. Answer the questions focusing on how you think, feel and react in these pressured situations.

Next, read each statement in sections A to H in the questionnaire and score yourself:

10 if it applies to you most of the time.

5 if it applies to you sometimes.

0 if it never or rarely applies to you.

I recommend you do this process quickly and instinctively. Avoid overthinking and trust your initial assessment as this will give you a more accurate result.

Then calculate the total score in each section and go to the end of the questionnaire to discover the mindset strategies that relate to each section, so you can create a prioritised list of strategies and chapters to read.

MINDSET STRATEGY QUESTIONNAIRE: SECTION A

Statement	Score
I worry about things I cannot control	10/5/0
I worry about making mistakes	10/5/0
I focus on achieving an outcome e.g. placing or win at competition	10/5/0

	Score
I worry about what people think of me	10/5/0
I focus on how well I'm riding	10/5/0
I struggle to remain focused	10/5/0
It's difficult to focus if I make a mistake	10/5/0
I think about what could go wrong	10/5/0
I think about whether I'm doing well	10/5/0

Total Score: ———

MINDSET STRATEGY QUESTIONNAIRE: SECTION B

Statement	Score
I often talk negatively to myself	10/5/0
I say negative things about myself to others	10/5/0
I beat myself up if things don't go well	10/5/0
I get frustrated if I make a mistake	10/5/0
I become irritable with people around me	10/5/0
I have very high expectations of myself	10/5/0
I doubt or question myself	10/5/0
I find it difficult to recover from setbacks	10/5/0
I don't congratulate myself when I ride well	10/5/0
I want to achieve perfection	10/5/0

Total Score: ———

MINDSET STRATEGY QUESTIONNAIRE: SECTION C

Statement	Score
I imagine worst case scenarios	10/5/0
I worry about what could go wrong	10/5/0
I worry about mistakes I've made in the past	10/5/0
I become anxious or stressed very quickly	10/5/0
Specific situations make me anxious/stressed	10/5/0
I freeze when I'm under pressure	10/5/0
I stop riding when I'm under pressure	10/5/0
It's difficult to ride positively consistently	10/5/0
I make the same mistakes repeatedly	10/5/0

Total Score: _____

MINDSET STRATEGY QUESTIONNAIRE: SECTION D

Statement	Score
I feel anxious or nervous	10/5/0
I get stressed	10/5/0
I feel under pressure	10/5/0
I struggle to control how I'm feeling	10/5/0
I notice my heart rate increasing	10/5/0
I notice that I hold my breath	10/5/0
I feel sick with worry / nerves	10/5/0

Statement	Score
I get annoyed or irritable with others	10/5/0
Anxiety and stress just creeps up on me	10/5/0
I freeze or stop riding	10/5/0

Total Score: _____

MINDSET STRATEGY QUESTIONNAIRE: SECTION E

Statement	Score
I have high expectations of myself	10/5/0
I doubt or question myself	10/5/0
I don't recognise when I've ridden well	10/5/0
I don't want to fail	10/5/0
I feel like I don't believe in myself	10/5/0
I beat myself up if I don't ride well	10/5/0
I worry about what people think of me	10/5/0
I don't like riding in front of an audience	10/5/0
I worry about doing my horse justice	10/5/0
I don't feel confident in myself	10/5/0

Total Score: _____

MINDSET STRATEGY QUESTIONNAIRE: SECTION F

Statement	Score
I feel unprepared	10/5/0
I struggle to ride well consistently	10/5/0
I'm not sure what my goals are	10/5/0
I don't feel like I learn from mistakes	10/5/0
I don't think I'm as skilled as other riders	10/5/0
I must achieve the outcome I want	10/5/0
I find practising new skills difficult	10/5/0
I have high expectations of myself	10/5/0
I don't know what I need to do to improve	10/5/0
I lack focus in my training plan	10/5/0

Total Score: _____

MINDSET STRATEGY QUESTIONNAIRE: SECTION G

Statement	Score
I feel out of control	10/5/0
I worry about what could go wrong	10/5/0
I find it difficult to maintain focus	10/5/0
I get distracted	10/5/0
I struggle to deal with pressure	10/5/0
I ride defensively	10/5/0

	Score
I become a passenger	10/5/0
I imagine worst case scenarios	10/5/0
I focus on what I don't want to happen	10/5/0
I worry about what other people think	10/5/0

Total Score: _____

MINDSET STRATEGY QUESTIONNAIRE: SECTION H

Statement	Score
I find it difficult to feel confident	10/5/0
I feel a sense of dread	10/5/0
I struggle to ride well consistently	10/5/0
I'm tense when I ride	10/5/0
I ride defensively	10/5/0
I freeze	10/5/0
I stop riding	10/5/0
I struggle to deal with the pressure	10/5/0
I struggle to control my nerves/stress	10/5/0

Total Score: _____

THE RESULTS ARE IN...

Now write your scores against the relevant sections below and then put the order of priority against each one according to the score, i.e. the highest scoring category will be 1, the second highest scoring category will be 2, etc. Once you have completed this, you will have a prioritized list of mindset strategies so you can read the chapters in the order that will work best for you.

Develop Positive Focus

Section A Score: _____   Priority: _____

Transform Your Inner Critic Into Your Best Supporter

Section B Score: _____   Priority: _____

Mental Rehearsal For Precision Riding

Section C Score: _____   Priority: _____

Master Your Emotions

Section D Score: _____   Priority: _____

How Beliefs Unlock Your Riding Potential

Section E Score: _____   Priority: _____

Performance Profiling to Optimise Your Results

Section F Score: _____   Priority: _____

Rituals & Routines To Boost Your Riding Performance

Section G Score: _____   Priority: _____

Develop Triggers To Unlock Performance Power

Section H Score: _____   Priority: _____

TAKING THE NEXT STEP

The choice is yours! You can start by reading the chapter that relates to your highest scoring mindset strategy, or if you want to learn more about how to deal with pressure and the key techniques to overcome the negative affects of pressure on the way you think, feel and ride, simply read the next chapter.

DECIDE HOW PRESSURE AFFECTS YOUR RIDING

Many riders find that pressure creates such stress that they are unable to perform at their best. Instead of thriving they struggle. Most of the time, riders do not notice the build up of pressure until it's too late. Whilst pressure is an inevitable result of challenging yourself and developing your riding skills, there are ways to manage pressure and use it to thrive so you can ride to the best of your ability.

If you compete then it's important to be aware that pressure is a natural feature of the competition environment because it's all about putting your skills to the test. In sports psychology, competitions are referred to as "open environments" because your performance and skills are scrutinised by both judges and spectators. This naturally increases the level of pressure that you feel in such an environment. There's nothing you can do to avoid feeling this increased pressure but you can control how it affects you.

When you take control of your thinking, you can control how you feel, enabling you to ride more positively and mentally prepare for any challenges.

When you use pressure to boost your motivation and focus, you may be surprised by how much easier it is to access your performance zone and ride more positively, improving your riding performance. When you allow pressure to make you anxious, nervous or stressed, your mindset will hold you back, making it almost impossible for you to ride at your best, often resulting in frustration and disappointment. This can become a repetitive negative cycle which can be very damaging to self-belief.

When I work with riders, I focus on helping them identify and make changes to how they think and how they react so they can use pressure to get in to their performance zone and boost their riding performance in everyday riding and at competitions.

FROM ZERO TO HERO

There is a massive difference in the mindset and performance outcomes of a rider who uses pressure positively, compared with a rider who feels anxious or stressed under pressure. However, it only takes a small number of mindset changes applied consistently to make this leap from disempowered to super-charged!

All riders need to experience some pressure to be able to perform at their best. It's just that many riders allow this pressure to build up, increasing beyond the point that they can manage and when this happens, riders get overwhelmed and stress shuts down their ability to ride well.

To transform pressure to power, you first need to make a decision that you're going to take control of how pressure affects you. Studies in psychology show that 90% of what happens in life is a result of our reactions to situations and only 10% is just what happens. You may have been surprised as you read that! It demonstrates that you have a lot more control over how pressure affects you and how you perform under pressure than you may have thought.

STAY PRESENT

You can only control what happens now, in this moment. You cannot control what happened a few seconds ago, a minute ago, a week ago, a year ago. You also cannot control what will happen in the future. By focusing your attention on controlling what happens in the present moment, you will be more able to influence your future outcomes.

WORRYING IS POINTLESS

Getting anxious truly is a waste of your energy. I'm not pointing this out so you beat yourself up about it, I'm simply pointing out that you have a choice about where you invest your energy. It takes just as much energy to worry as it does to focus positively. So make a choice to invest energy in being positive rather than fixating on your concerns and worries.

Worrying about how you'll ride won't make you ride better because all you'll do is switch on the part of your brain that makes you anxious and, once you get into that state, it is difficult to calm down and refocus. This often results in riders feeling overwhelmed.

ACTION

Examine what you worry about when you ride, whether you find yourself experiencing pressure in everyday riding or at competitions. What is it that triggers your negative thoughts? What reasons do you have for these worrying negative thoughts? This will help you determine if the reason is a genuine safety concern or something outside your control (e.g. worrying about what other people are thinking about you).

If it is a genuine safety concern, I recommend you develop an action plan to deal with it. There's no point worrying about something to do with your personal safety when you can take action to deal with it. If it's outside your control, focus on using relaxation techniques and changing your thinking habits to reduce your stress level and enable you to create positive focus.

Make a choice to focus your energy positively on the task in hand. If you're struggling to work out how to do this because you've got a lot of negative beliefs or habits, you'll find the chapters on beliefs, inner critic and positive focus particularly helpful.

CHANGE YOUR THINKING

You may already be aware that your actions determine your results because you'll see this cause and effect relationship happening when you ride and compete. You may also know that to get different results you need to change what you do and how you think. You may already know how to improve your horse's way of going, get him/her focused and perform well. What you may be finding difficult is putting all your technical riding skills and knowledge in to practice when you're under pressure. You may know what you need to do, but doing it when you are anxious or stressed is very difficult.

What you may not know is that our brains are wired so that we behave in a way that is consistent with our beliefs, values and thinking.

So unless you're prepared to change your thinking, your actions won't fundamentally change, which means you will find it difficult to improve your riding performance and outcomes in everyday riding and at competition. One rider I worked with was so committed to changing her thinking that she progressed from having regular stops during the cross country phase to consistently going clear inside the time within one month. Whilst every chapter in this book has valuable tools and techniques, they will only make a positive difference to your riding when you apply them consistently.

This book will show you how to set clear goals that are directly related to your ability to control your riding performance and influence your horse to work in partnership with you. Goals that focus you on the process of riding, the task that you need to complete, rather than the outcome or performance level you wish to achieve, will be much more effective in creating positive focus that enables you to ride at your best.

HOME FROM HOME

Riders who struggle to deal with the pressure of the competition environment are often frustrated because they know they are capable of performing at a higher level. This doesn't come from being overconfident or arrogant; it comes from experiencing a drop in their performance level at competitions, compared with their performance level at home. Some riders report that their riding becomes awkward and clumsy at competitions, whereas everything flows much better and feels easier at home. This is because the pressure of the competition environment gets the better of them.

The mindset strategies in this book will enable you to reduce this performance differential between home and competition and improve your competition performance, so that you are more able to transfer that level of skill that you see and feel at home to the competition environment.

MANAGE IT EARLY

When pressure builds to unmanageable and overwhelming levels, it is often because riders have not recognised the early signs that their stress level is increasing above a level that is helpful, creating anxiety, negative thinking and nerves. Whilst you need to experience a level of stress to get into your performance zone so you can focus on using your skills to ride at your best, when your stress level increases beyond this optimal level, it starts to have a detrimental effect on your performance.

Many riders are unaware of their optimal stress level and as a result they are also unaware of when pressure starts to get too much. They are unable to identify the early warning signs, which means they are unable to manage their stress level effectively. Most of the time they don't realise that pressure has built to an overwhelming level until it's too late. By the time they notice it, their stress level is way above what they need to ride at their best.

As I've already mentioned, pressure can either have a positive or negative effect on your riding. The key to managing the effects of pressure on your performance so that you benefit from it, is to know the level of pressure you need to ride at your best and then watch out for early warning signs that pressure is beginning to increase your stress above the optimal level for you.

ACTION

If you and I were working together, we would complete a stress profiling exercise to establish your optimal stress level, determine at what points you need relaxation techniques to reduce your stress level and which techniques would work best to set you up for success. To take the first step to become more aware of your optimal stress level and what triggers an increase in your stress level, I recommend you complete the following exercise.

Think about a time when you rode well. On a scale of 1-10, how much stress were you experiencing? 1 = so relaxed you're almost asleep, 10 = extremely nervous, anxious (panic) or stressed. Whatever your score is, this is your optimal level of stress. Everyone's level of optimal stress is different so there are no right or wrong answers!

Now consider a time when you've not ridden well, it could be in training or at a competition, perhaps when you made a mistake or just didn't ride to the best of your ability. Score your stress level again using the scale of 1 to 10.

Although I don't know your specific scores, it is normal to experience a higher level of stress when you've not ridden well compared with when you've ridden at your best.

It's important to examine the difference between your optimal stress score and the level of stress you experience when you do not ride well. Closing the gap between the two and reducing your stress level is a key first step to improving

PERFORMANCE PROFILING TO OPTIMISE YOUR RESULTS

If you have a stretching or ambitious goal that you really want to achieve, the process of transforming pressure into power starts with reducing uncertainty to improve your confidence and belief in your skills, capability and performance level. Performance profiling is a key tool developed by sports psychologists that has been tried and tested across many sports at all levels, from amateur to professional and world champions. The reason performance profiling is so widely used is because it enables you to get clarity on the key areas of your performance where a small improvement will make a big difference to your results.

It enables you to measure your current performance and skill level, then compare it against the level of performance required to achieve your objectives. For example, if you event, your goal may be to go double clear and inside the time cross-country, or if you're a dressage rider, it may be to achieve a particular score. Where there are gaps between your current level of performance and the required level of performance, the profiling process allows you to clearly see the size of each performance gap and focus on the key priority areas to improve your skills and capability. This enables you to plan the steps you need to take to close the gap between where you are now and achieving your goal.

PRECISION PERFORMANCE

If you don't currently profile your performance, you may find it difficult to pinpoint the exact areas where you need to improve. Often riders hope that if they simply practice more, they'll be able to make the improvements they want. But unless you're precise in your approach to, how you practise and what you practise, you'll find it difficult to make precise improvements in your riding performance.

When you complete the performance profiling process, you'll be able to identify and address gaps in your current riding performance level. It's an objective measure of performance and will enable you to identify the specific skills and techniques you need to improve on to achieve the performance level you desire.

Performance profiling works by assessing your current performance level and comparing that against the level of performance you need to achieve your goals. It's useful to think of a rider you admire, who is currently achieving the level of performance you want, when when considering the level of performance you require.

Performance profiling is a key performance enhancement tool that enables you to gain greater control over your riding performance, and if you have ambitions to move up the levels or become a successful professional rider, it is essential that you start using performance profiling.

Whether you're looking to step up to the next level of competition or simply looking to improve your riding performance at your current level, performance profiling will help you to analyse the skills needed to improve and actions required to achieve those improvements.

ACTION

Complete all the steps in this chapter to complete your performance profile. If you're competing, make sure you do this when you have at least 2 weeks before your next competition. If you're a few days away from a competition, wait until you have more time to complete this process. Performance profiling is particularly helpful for planning your practise over the winter period.

STEP 1: GET CLEAR ON YOUR GOALS

To get the most out of performance profiling it is really important that you clarify your goals and what really motivates you, because without motivation and clear goals, it is extremely difficult to identify and take forward the improvements so you continually learn and grow your skills to ride at your best.

We only ride at our best when we are motivated to do so; this is especially true in equestrian sport, a sport well known for its highs and lows.

Your ability to be mentally resilient and overcome setbacks is critical. Remember that it is not the absence of challenge that makes someone mentally resilient; it is their ability to overcome challenges and remain focused on their goals, changing their plan and refocusing their efforts when their original plan does not work out. Part of the reason that some riders are better at this than others is their level of motivation. If you are highly motivated to achieve the goals that you have set for yourself, the likelihood is you will find a way to do that, and you will be prepared to experiment to find another way to achieve your goals.

Write down the riding and competing goals that make you feel really excited and motivated. Visualise what you will see, hear and feel once you've achieved these goals. Think about what the best thing will be about achieving each goal.

Once you're clear about the goals that motivate you, it's important to state your goals in a way that will make it more likely that you will achieve them. There are several tests that you can apply when you have written your goals. Review each of your goals against the following criteria and adjust your goal statements as required:

Specific – make sure the goal specifically states what you want to achieve. Avoid generic statements like "I want to do well."

Challenging – make your goals stretching so you have something to aim for as this will build your confidence as you improve your skills and performance.

Controllable – focus on your performance level like jumping a clear round, rather than on results and outcomes. Whilst it's great to have ambitions to achieve specific results, it's more important to have performance goals because these are the goals that you have greater control over and can measure. Performance goals will enable you to focus on what you need to do when you ride to give yourself the best possible chance of success.

Attainable – your goals should be something you can aim to achieve within the next 3, 6 or 12 months. Working towards longer-term goals makes it more difficult to work out the precise steps you need to take to improve your performance. Goal setting and performance profiling should be something you do on a regular basis, ideally every 3 months, so once you've achieved your short term goals and improved your riding performance, you simply define your next set of goals and assess your improved level of performance against those new goals.

Measurable – goals must be measurable so you can track how you're doing, so you know how much progress you're making and so that you also know when you've achieved your goals. This is key to helping you build confidence as you progress towards the achievement of your goals.

Personal – your goals must reflect what you want and your personal ambitions. If you work towards a goal because someone else has told you that you should, you won't have the motivation and determination needed to achieve it. Make sure that the goal is truly something you want.

As you progress and achieve your goals, you'll be able to take confidence from your successes which will help you to build on your achievements and further improve your performance. When you get the goal setting process right, you can create a virtuous circle of success and confidence, so investing time in defining and stating your goals is vitally important. I recommend you create and work towards 1 to 3 goals at a time.

STEP 2: COMPLETE YOUR PERFORMANCE PROFILE

The first part of the performance profile is the performance criteria. These are the measures that you will use to assess your riding performance. These criteria need to measure the factors that contribute to your ability to achieve your goals. Here are some of the performance criteria I use to help riders assess their performance:

- Ability to keep rhythm

- Seeing distances

- Working the horse in an outline

- Balance

- Coordination

- Relaxation

- Riding positively

- Ability to focus

- Maintaining a positive outlook

- Ability to refocus quickly following a distraction or mistake

- Ability to overcome setbacks

The second part of the performance profile is the Importance Score. This means that you need to score how important each of the performance criteria are in enabling you to achieve your goals. That's why it's absolutely essential that you define your goals first before completing a performance profile, so if you've not completed the action outlined earlier in this chapter, do it now! To score importance, use a scale of 1 to 10 where 1 is not important at all and 10 is critical.

Once you've worked through the performance criteria and assigned an importance score to each one, you're ready to move on and assess your current performance. When you do this, you need to be calm and ready to review your performance rationally and objectively. Only complete this assessment when you are able to do this and can dedicate time to really think about your current riding performance. If you're stressed out or have other priorities that are distracting you, wait until you are calm and thinking clearly before completing this step.

If you're ready to complete this step, take each criteria in turn and score your current performance level on a scale of 1 to 10 where 1 is poor, 5 is average and 10 is excellent. Think about how well you can perform each criterion right now because that will indicate your level of skill and will help you to determine an appropriate score. At this stage you're just focusing on your current performance and skill level.

Once you have assessed your current performance level and scored yourself out of 10 for each criterion, the next step is to score each criterion based on how well you need to perform it to achieve your goals. This is the Required Score. To assess this, you will need to consider the level of skill you need to achieve your goals; you may wish to think about a rider you admire who is currently achieving the results you want. If you find this step difficult, you will find it helpful to ask your instructor or coach for some guidance. Remember they may not be familiar with this process but they may be able to advise you on the level of performance you need to achieve your goals.

Once you have completed the profile, you'll be able to identify the key steps required to achieve your goals.

STEP 3: IDENTIFY YOUR PRIORITIES

It is important that you review the scores in your performance profile to prioritise the areas for improvement. This will help you create a clear plan of action with steps to achieve your goals.

To determine the priorities, make the following calculation:

Required Score – Current Score = Performance Gap

Performance Gap x Importance Score = Priority Score

This makes the process of identifying your key priorities much simpler; just rank each of the criteria in order, starting with the criterion that has the highest priority score.

Next, look at the top three priority areas and identify the actions you need to take to improve your riding performance in these three areas. If you identify lots of actions, just focus on the first step you need to take to make an improvement in your performance and to develop your skills further. Write down the actions you will take and the date that you aim to achieve each one. I recommend you document these actions on a large piece of paper and put it somewhere where you can see it on a daily basis so you can remind yourself each day of the commitments you've made to improve your riding performance.

When I work with riders, I focus on helping them to identify both the key priorities and also the quick wins from their completed performance profile. When riders are able to achieve quick wins and boost their performance quickly, they gain confidence and focus, which builds momentum to make more changes to improve their performance.

STEP 4: PRECISION PRACTISE

To gain maximum value from this process, it is essential that you implement the actions you've identified from your top three priorities accurately and consistently. Whether you're refining existing skills or learning new ones, it is important that you dedicate yourself to practising regularly and consistently. Practise makes permanent!

To be effective, practise must be purposeful and focused. It's not just about the number of hours of practise, it's about the quality. Research shows that to become world class in any sport, you need ten thousand hours of purposeful practise. To be purposeful, practise must be focused on making improvements and not just focusing on the things you find easy. This means you have to be motivated and committed to making changes to improve your skills, so you can ride to the best of your ability. You need to continually focus on what you want, how to get there and believe in yourself.

Precision practise means being dedicated to practising the elements that you find difficult and you know you need to improve to achieve your goals. This can include both psychological elements, (e.g. relaxation, focus) as well as technical elements, (e.g. flying changes, related distances). If you invest your time in practising movements, transitions, shapes or jumps you find easy, you will not improve your overall performance. To improve performance it's important to master the elements of your riding discipline that you find difficult.

To help you structure your practice sessions, I recommend you spend 80% of the time in each session focusing on areas for improvement and 20% of the time focusing on elements that you find easy and enjoy, so that you make progress more quickly, whilst achieving a balance between difficult and easy activities. If what you need to improve is something that your horse finds equally difficult, it is important that you take this into account when you practise, so that you give your horse sufficient breaks to help them process what they have learnt.

Ultimately your ability to improve your riding performance is determined by your willingness to work outside your comfort zone and learn, so you can focus on the elements you need to improve in order to perform to the best of your ability and potential. The concept of working outside the comfort zone is widely misunderstood and is something rider's often struggle with, so I've dedicated a section to this topic at the end of this chapter to explain how to take positive steps to work outside your comfort zone.

STEP 5: SET YOUR EXPECTATIONS

A key part of the performance profiling process is being clear about the expectations you have of yourself. Many riders I work with set such high expectations that they set themselves up for disappointment, and when they don't meet those exceptionally high and unrealistic expectations they believe they have failed. When this happens, you can lose confidence and motivation, and it can be tempting to give up.

So it's vital to set realistic expectations so that you focus on making improvements step by step. When you achieve small improvements regularly you'll find you soon build confidence, focus and greater motivation to keep striving to achieve your goals. Remember that performance profiling is a powerful tool that enables you to achieve your goals, and in order to achieve your goals you must be motivated and committed. Make sure you set reasonable expectations for your rate of progress and performance improvement.

STEP 6: REVIEW & ADJUST

Once you have set clear and realistic expectations for your riding performance level and rate of progress, it's important to measure your performance so you can track and celebrate progress. If you compete, it is best to focus on reviewing your performance after you have completed the competition. Doing it at a competition will only distract you and take your focus away from the present moment. It's critical that you remain in the present moment at a competition, so wait until you have returned home before measuring your performance.

Remember that the best analysis is done when you are calm and able to think objectively, so make sure you are in the right state of mind and ready to review your performance.

First, make a list of what went well. You will find it useful to refer to the performance criteria in your performance profile and score yourself against each criterion, based on how well you believe you achieved it.

Then focus in on what you need to improve and work out how to improve it. To help you focus on the key learning points from situations (e.g. lesson, competition, schooling session) that did not go to plan, here are some useful questions you can ask yourself:

- What specifically did not go to plan?
- How did it happen? What happened in the moments before the problem occurred?
- What were your immediate thoughts? How did they influence you?
- What happened next?
- What are the positives you can take away from this experience?
- What have you learned from this experience?
- What will you do differently next time?
- What could you practise to overcome the problem you experienced?

These are some of the questions I use when I work with riders who have had a setback to help them bounce back more quickly and focus on what they can do to improve their performance.

What you learn from any situation depends on your interpretation, and there are multiple interpretations of the same situation. If you find yourself interpreting a situation really negatively, ask yourself "What else could this situation mean?" Find something, anything that's positive. It's important that you take a balanced view of every situation. There are both positives and negatives you can take from any situation.

Once you've completed your performance review, make a list of the actions you can take to achieve further improvements in your riding performance. Then compare these against the actions you've already identified as priorities in your performance profile and reprioritise where appropriate to incorporate the new actions and create an updated prioritised action list.

Whilst it's good to have a clear list of actions, avoid focusing on lots of actions simultaneously. This creates pressure and makes it more difficult to learn. Your conscious mind, which is the part of your brain that helps you to learn, works best when you only focus on one thing at a time. So remember to keep it simple and focus on the most important actions, one at a time.

Achieving your riding goals becomes more possible when you focus on continuous self-improvement and focused practise. Dedication to continuous learning will enable you to build your skills and improve your riding performance, which will help to grow your confidence so you can achieve the results you want in everyday riding, training and at competition.

A dressage rider who believed that she would never good enough to achieve her goals...

She came to me because she was feeling disheartened after years of berating herself, because she wasn't achieving perfection. She was surrounded by professional riders in her local area who were producing highly competitive horses and achieving strong test scores. She told me that she felt that she had failed because she wasn't achieving the same test quality or score as the professional riders.

I pointed out that berating herself for not achieving the same results as professional riders would not help her achieve her goals. Whilst she understood from our discussion that comparing herself to the professional riders was unfair, she still had a strong desire to make significant improvements to her test riding. She felt she was not capable of making the improvements required to produce the quality of test she wanted. We created a performance profile to help her prioritise the areas for improvement and identified actions, so she could focus on the key steps required to enhance the quality of her test riding. By focusing on these priorities, she was able to take a more balanced perspective and told me she felt more positive about the path to achieving her goals.

STEP 7: PLAN FOR YOUR NEXT CHALLENGE

Whether you're planning a competition, a training event or a solo hack, confidence and composure in challenging situations comes from doing the right practise and being prepared.

It is important to focus on taking small steps forward each time you ride and compete to improve your performance and achieve your goals. When planning your next challenge, make sure you set an achievable goal and create a plan of what you need to improve to achieve it. Then track your performance against your plan.

Whether your chosen challenge is a competition, training event or hack, I recommend you create a plan to help you mentally prepare for the challenge ahead. When you create your plan, think about the unexpected things that you may encounter based on your previous experiences and consider how you could deal with each of these factors to gain as much control as possible. When you plan for the unexpected, it means you have a contingency plan that you can use if you need to, and this will give you a greater sense of control and improve your confidence.

Once you've created a plan, stick to it! If you have anyone coming to support you at a clinic, training event or competition, make sure they know that you have a plan and that you need to stick to it. Use the plan to focus on what is important to avoid getting distracted by elements you cannot control. Read your plan regularly in advance of your planned challenge and on the day before you ride, to help you remember what you need to focus on to achieve your goal.

LOVE YOUR LEARNING ZONE

The concept of being outside your comfort zone is one that is widely misunderstood. Many riders don't understand the difference between the zones that sit outside the comfort zone: the learning zone and the fear zone.

Whilst you may be aware that being in your comfort zone feels easy, you are probably less aware of how far you need to be outside your comfort zone in order to learn and improve. The short answer is that you don't need to actually be that far outside your comfort zone. You just need to be far enough out to feel uncomfortable!

So if you are in a situation where you feel challenged and stretched and still able to make decisions and adjust your riding, you are in your learning zone. You may make mistakes and it may feel awkward at times, but you can adjust your riding accordingly and learn from it.

If you're in a situation where you feel scared and your confidence is low, you've gone too far outside your comfort zone. What's happened is you've gone past your learning zone and into your fear zone. Some of the riders I work with push themselves across into the fear zone in the belief that this is how they will be able to learn and improve more quickly.

Whilst it's important to set yourself stretching challenges, when you're in your fear zone you cannot learn effectively. When we become scared or anxious, our fight/flight response takes control and the part of our brain responsible for rational thinking and learning shuts down, unable to function properly.

Many riders acknowledge the importance of this in training their horses and yet do not realise that the same holds true for humans. A horse cannot learn if it is scared or too far out of its comfort zone, and so most riders approach training their horses in a way that ensures that they learn and they embed new skills. It's important that you apply the same logic and understanding to yourself to set yourself up for success.

Purposeful practise will feel uncomfortable at times but it's a sign that you're making progress. Whilst being in your comfort zone creates a nice comfortable feeling, continually being in your comfort zone does not enable you to grow and improve your riding skills and performance. You need to be in your learning zone to grow and improve.

Being in your learning zone means you will be more able to think and work through problems. If you end up in your fear zone, you'll lose that ability to solve problems and make corrections. Everyone learns at a different pace, so just work out the pace you need to learn at. Remember that every improvement is a success so celebrate it!

Being aware of the specific areas you need to improve is incredibly important. I cannot emphasise enough how important it is, so take a moment to feel good about about knowing precisely what it is that you need to improve because it gives you a clear roadmap for how you will improve your riding performance, your horse's performance and ultimately achieve your goals.

HOW BELIEFS UNLOCK YOUR PERFORMANCE POTENTIAL

Do you believe with absolute certainty that you've got what it takes to achieve your goals? It's one thing having goals, it's quite another to believe in your ability to achieve them. Having a strong belief in your skill and ability to ride at your best when you are under pressure is essential to being able to ride positively and achieve the outcomes you want.

Self-belief and self-confidence are inextricably linked. You cannot have one without the other. Once you build self-belief, you gain greater confidence and this grows your self-belief, and so the virtuous circle continues building more and more belief in your skill and ability as a rider.

Many riders associate self-belief and confidence with overconfidence and even arrogance. So when they ride well, particularly when they achieve a good result at competition, they praise the horse and take very little credit themselves. Whilst world class riders will often do this publicly, they will almost certainly acknowledge and celebrate their success in private. They know very well the part they played in producing the winning performance and have built such self-belief and confidence in their ability, that it does not impact them psychologically when they graciously and modestly accept their success in public.

If you do not yet have this level of self-belief and confidence, it is important that you take time to celebrate every success, no matter how small, because it will help you to build your confidence. The performance profiling strategy I shared in the previous chapter will help you with this process.

It is important that we deal with the myth that self-belief and confidence result in arrogance. Arrogance can only occur when someone's assessment of their own ability far outweighs their actual ability, and they become complacent about their performance because they have overvalued and overrated their skills. People who indulge in arrogance see no reason to continually learn and improve because in their mind they are already more than good enough! In the case of every single rider I have worked with to date, it is far more common that they significantly undervalue and underrate their ability and skill level. In every case, they have achieved far more than they are prepared to acknowledge, and it makes them feel uncomfortable to acknowledge the true extent of their skill and ability. This means that they lack belief and confidence, and because often they have been underestimating their skill and ability for a long time, they find it difficult to break free from it.

Much of the work I do with riders focuses on changing their perception and beliefs about their skills and abilities.

So in this chapter, we're going to examine the process of belief change to help you overcome negative beliefs and build greater confidence.

PERSONAL POWER

When you believe something with absolute certainty, it becomes a self-fulfilling prophecy. These self-fulfilling prophecies either empower you to take action and remain resilient when things get tough, or they disempower you, stripping you of motivation, persistence and control over your performance.

Positive, empowering beliefs give you greater control, enabling you to focus and control your emotions when you ride so you can perform at your best. These beliefs also support you in learning and improving because you will be more open to constructive feedback and able to learn important lessons when things do not go to plan.

Negative, disempowering beliefs take away your personal power and although they may stay hidden beneath the surface of your conscious mind most of the time, when you are faced with a challenging situation, they surface and start causing chaos, raising your stress levels and making you feel overwhelmed. They are also responsible for making you doubt yourself and for fixing your focus on things you cannot control when you ride and compete, which means that you feel less in control of your riding and you are more likely to make mistakes.

Everybody is watching me, I can't do this...

The biggest issue I encounter in coaching sessions is the difficulty riders have believing in themselves. I worked with a dressage rider who had trained hard to develop her horse from a quirky, unbacked youngster to an affiliated dressage horse. Yet she felt that she didn't deserve to compete him. I listened to her as she described how she feared people watching her ride her test and how unfocused she would become in the warm-up when she realised that professional riders were competing in her class. I was stunned by how she overlooked her achievements; she had trained her horse from unbacked to qualifying for the Regional Championship and yet this didn't seem to give her confidence. As we talked, I observed that she sounded confused and defeated. I highlighted the disconnect between how she felt about herself as a rider and her achievements, pointing out that she was a skilled and capable rider. As we explored this further, it became clear that her confidence was fragile because she lacked self-belief, which meant she could not consistently ride positively at competitions. Her test scores were variable as a result. As soon as she competed at venues where professional riders were competing in her class or people she knew were spectating, she lost confidence, focus and important test marks. We discussed ways to build her self-belief through reinforcing and strengthening positive beliefs on a daily basis, so that she could be more confident and focused when she competed. Four weeks after the session, she and her horse won their affiliated dressage class. In the months that followed, she consistently achieved competitive test scores and was placed at several competitions.

MIND MECHANICS

First it's important that you get familiar with the mechanics of how your mind uses your beliefs, so you can understand how to challenge them.

The reason beliefs play such an important role in your ability to ride at your best, is because of how our brain processes information. It is a mechanical process that starts with our subconscious mind, which processes every single last piece of information that we see, hear and feel. Right now, and in every second after that, your subconscious mind is processing thousands of pieces of information, from your heartbeat to the weather outside. Whilst your subconscious mind has an almost unlimited capacity for processing information, your conscious mind has a much more limited capacity, only able to focus on one or two things at a time.

When you try to divide your attention between multiple things, the quality of your focus decreases because your conscious mind cannot cope. In other words, your subconscious mind is the master of multi-tasking, unlike your conscious mind. This is why some people get confused about multi-tasking. Multi-tasking only really happens where you are using skills stored subconsciously, alongside your conscious focus. It's like when you're riding and you instinctively know when to adjust your position before, during and after a jump. This is because you've practised it so much, it's become embedded in your subconscious and now it takes no effort to execute. This means you can focus your conscious attention on something else, such as the line to the fence.

So how does information flow through from your subconscious mind to your conscious mind? Well first of all, your subconscious mind needs some rules in order to process and sort through all the data it is processing, so it can identify the items that are most important and bring those to your attention. Your beliefs are part of that rulebook that your subconscious mind uses to filter everything you see, hear and feel. This means that your beliefs determine how you interpret situations, what you learn, how you feel about yourself and ultimately how you ride under pressure.

Because everyone's beliefs are different, their brains are operating different filtering systems, and that means that everyone's perception and interpretation of reality is also different. When you change your beliefs, you change your reality! Some riders find this a bit mind-blowing, and really it is, because when you realise that you can take greater control over your reality by changing your beliefs, you open up a whole new world of opportunity to unlock your riding potential.

CHANGING YOUR BELIEFS

So how do you go about changing beliefs? The first step is to challenge them with evidence that contradicts the belief. To show you how to do this, I'm going to give you an example of the common belief about the role of natural talent in determining rider success and then I'm going to give you a summary of evidence that will help change your belief about natural talent.

THE BELIEF

Many of the ambitious riders I work with believe that unless they have natural talent, they won't ever make it as a professional or world class rider. When you believe this, you will be less motivated and determined to reach your goal. Every time you encounter a setback, you will interpret it as a sign of failure, and confirmation of your belief that you do not have natural talent. This is the way our beliefs work. The more we believe something, the more our subconscious presents us with evidence that our belief is correct, even if there is evidence to the contrary, and this further reinforces the belief. Your brain doesn't distinguish between empowering and disempowering beliefs; it just reinforces the beliefs you hold.

THE CHALLENGE

This is one of the beliefs that I am very well positioned to challenge, having studied with world class geneticists during my degree at Oxford University. The reality is that human genetics remains a bit of a mystery. Even now, we still don't fully understand all of the genetic code which every human has, and the area where we have the least understanding is how our genes influence and determine our behaviour. Even when scientists think they have discovered a gene that determines behaviour or success in a particular area of life like business or sport, it is so difficult to prove the link in a scientifically rigorous way that, at best, these genetic links are just educated guesses. Most of the time it is incredibly difficult to separate genetic causes from environmental causes.

Secondly, if you think about how quickly athletes can run a mile now compared with 50 years ago, it is crazy. Whereas Roger Bannister's 4 minute mile became famous for being the world record, it has since been broken many times over, and now there are teenagers in secondary and high schools who can run 4 minute miles. This quick progression in our ability to run 1 mile more quickly has not happened as a result of genetics. Believe me, evolution doesn't happen that fast! It has happened because we have developed a better understanding of how to run well, we have better running technology in the form of running shoes, we are able to analyse diet and fitness better and we are more able as a result to design training programmes that focus on the precise skills that athletes need to develop in order to run faster.

Finally, there are examples everywhere of athletes who are not, genetically speaking, well designed for their sports. One example is Usain Bolt whose long legs do not make him ideally designed for running short distances fast. Despite not being ideally designed for his chosen sport, he has adapted his techniques and is extremely successful as a result.

So now you can see how to challenge a negative belief, and if you currently hold a belief about natural talent, I hope that this has started to change your mind and your perspective.

MAKING THE CHANGE

Even just accepting this evidence will help you to start breaking this limiting belief down and replace it with a new more empowering belief. Once you've challenged a negative belief you'll be much more able to overcome it and realise that you have a choice in what you believe. In this example, when you choose to believe that professional and world class riders are there because of dedication, hard work and many thousands of hours of purposeful practise (remember it takes ten thousand hours to become world class), your subconscious mind will start to filter based on this belief, and you will suddenly find that you become more inspired and motivated to achieve your goal. You will think of ideas to overcome setbacks and challenges more readily and you will be more determined to succeed, so you will be more able to cope with the highs and lows of riding and competing.

It is common to discover negative beliefs that are out of date. Unless you have consciously examined and challenged your beliefs in the past, it's unlikely that you will have cleared out the old stuff! Because this exercise is not something we are taught to do, our beliefs are not regularly updated throughout our lives, and we can carry beliefs around with us that we have had for a very long time. Riders who struggle with self belief are often working off an old rulebook of beliefs that they've been holding since they were young, and because they have not consciously updated them and challenged them they still hold onto those even though their current reality is actually quite different. This is why beliefs are so powerful. Our reality can change and be completely different but, because we have old beliefs, we still use old filters to interpret and respond to situations.

ACTION

This is a belief brainstorming exercise! Write down everything you believe about yourself and your skills as a rider. Examine each of the beliefs in turn and tick the ones that empower you and enable you to ride at your best, then put a cross against each of the beliefs that have a limiting or negative effect on your mindset, self-confidence and riding performance. Allow yourself 24 hours to complete this exercise because sometimes beliefs that we are not very aware of can surface after your initial brainstorm.

Remember this is an exercise about your perceptions of yourself, and these perceptions and beliefs determine how you interpret situations and particularly how you deal with setbacks. That means there are no right or wrong answers!

Next, work through each of your negative beliefs and identify evidence that contradicts each of these beliefs. To search for this evidence, reflect on your own experience and knowledge, things people have said to you and things you've noticed or observed whilst watching other riders.

Finally, replace the negative beliefs with an alternative, positive belief that will empower you and enable you to perform at your best when you compete. Identify evidence that supports your new positive beliefs. Again, search for evidence wherever you can. It will be there somewhere; it just may be buried because your subconscious mind will not have been filtering for evidence to support the new beliefs. If your new positive belief is something you've not yet been able to demonstrate, that's OK. Just make sure you write it down, in the present tense, and remind yourself of it frequently. You could replace an old belief of "I'm not a very good rider" or "I lack confidence in my ability as a rider" with "I am becoming a more confident rider." You might not feel that yet, but say it to yourself often enough and you'll start to make a shift in your belief and your confidence level.

Remember that, as yet, your new belief is not part of the rulebook that your subconscious mind is using to filter data and present you with your version of reality. This means you are going to need to consciously override the old negative belief and replace it with your new positive belief, many times, to score it from the rulebook and install the new positive belief instead. Every time you notice an old negative belief, immediately replace it with your new belief. When you do this, you'll start to notice new evidence or you will remember something from your experience that supports your new belief. Write this down and remind yourself of it regularly. If you do this consistently, every day for at least 2 weeks, you will start to notice a difference. Eventually, you won't need to do this any more because you will have been able to overwrite the old negative belief and your brain will have accepted the new positive belief. You need to do this consistently though, and practise it in order to build your new belief and make it stick!

As you progress, it is very important that you continue to review and challenge your beliefs because as you develop and refine your skills, you will need to change your beliefs to keep up with your changing reality.

TURN IT UP!

Negative beliefs can easily overpower your positive, empowering beliefs and this is why they have the power to control your riding performance in pressurized situations (e.g. competition, training event with a young horse). When you are under pressure, these negative beliefs rise to the surface and override any positive, empowering beliefs you have.

That's why it is vital to power up your positive beliefs by giving them more attention and focus than your negative beliefs.

ACTION

Revisit your list of beliefs and this time focus on your list of positive, empowering beliefs. Transfer this list to a place where you can easily see and review it every day. You can use a notebook, poster or phone. Write down your beliefs and remind yourself of the evidence that backs them up. Then, twice a day every day for 2 weeks, read them aloud, ideally while looking in the mirror. This is the best way to strengthen positive beliefs. If you feel uncomfortable about doing that, you can just read them to yourself without reading them aloud. Reading them frequently is essential. It will only take you a few minutes every day, so just work out when you will do it and then just do it! If you prefer, you can record them on your phone using a voice recording app and play it regularly so you can hear yourself saying your positive beliefs.

MENTAL REHEARSAL FOR PRECISION PERFORMANCE

You may not be aware of it, but mental rehearsal is something you probably do on a regular basis. It's just that you probably are not consciously using it to improve your riding performance. In fact, most of the time, we use mental rehearsal to get anxious, nervous or stressed out. So in this chapter I'm going to explain what mental rehearsal is and how you can use it to improve your riding performance. When you use mental rehearsal correctly, you'll be able to use it to ride more positively and achieve better results.

Whilst this skill is regularly used by riders competing at the highest level across dressage, eventing and showjumping, it is a skill that everyone can develop. In this chapter I will be sharing my top tips to help you improve and develop greater positive mental rehearsal power.

HEADING FOR A FALL

Many riders use mental rehearsal to focus on all the things that could go wrong and hold them back from achieving the performance level and result they want. They play a series of images or a movie over and over in their mind before they ride or compete, which not only increases their stress levels, but also sends a message to their brain that this set of images or movie is what they want! The human brain is easily influenced by images, so the more you imagine something, the more your brain attempts to recreate those images and movies in real life.

You should think about your brain being like Google. Just like Google, the human brain functions best when you give it precise, specific instructions and keywords. It then goes on a search to locate the information you have requested. The more specific and precise the instruction, the more quickly it produces the answers you are looking for.

Your brain also does not distinguish between real and vividly imagined experience, so whether you are imagining something going wrong at a competition or actually in that situation for real, your brain will treat both as if they are real!

This means that when you practise negative mental rehearsal and you run worst case scenarios through your mind, you not only create vivid images and movies, you also create the thoughts and feelings that go with that scenario so you become tense and anxious. So although you are only using your imagination to think about a situation, you become so immersed that you respond as if you are in that situation right now!

That is why negative mental rehearsal can have such a devastating effect on your riding, because if you imagine your horse stopping at a fence or spooking at something enough times, you are instructing your brain to create that situation. Also, when you mentally rehearse in this way, you are building an association between being in a particular situation (e.g. just before a particular jump), thinking stressful thoughts and feeling anxious, nervous or stressed.

This means that when you face that situation, your brain will recognise the situation as one that requires you to feel anxious, nervous or stressed and will automatically trigger an increase in your stress levels which will make you more tense and less likely to ride positively. So what you feared would happen, does happen! This reinforces your negative mental rehearsal and makes the images even more vivid, which means that the cycle of negative mental rehearsal continues.

Some riders find it difficult to break free from this cycle because negative mental rehearsal becomes a habit and therefore they are often not aware that they are stuck in this cycle. However, being aware that this is happening is the first and most important step to breaking the habit.

REHEARSAL IS PRACTISE

Mental rehearsal is also a form of practise that complements your ridden practise. Because your brain does not differentiate between real and imagined experience, you can continue practising even once you've untacked your horse, and refine your skills remotely!

When you practise negative mental rehearsal, your practise is focused on not using your skills effectively and not riding to the best of your ability.

For mental rehearsal to be effective as practise, it is vital that it is very specific and clear. It must be tailored to you, your riding aims and your key areas for improvement. When I devise a mental rehearsal plan and create personalized audio recordings, I work with the rider to identify a specific skill or aspect of their riding that they want to improve.

RELEASING THE HANDBRAKE

Negative mental rehearsal prevents you from riding at your best. You need to think of it like a handbrake because it blocks your performance. It does not allow you to take calculated risks or make quick decisions. It slows you down and holds you back!

When you make a shift from negative mental rehearsal to positive mental rehearsal, you release the handbrake on your performance and even just one small change in your mental rehearsal habits can make a big difference. Positive mental rehearsal has the power to build your confidence, motivation and resilience. It helps you master your emotions, maintain positive focus and gets you ready for being in your performance zone.

So if you struggle to ride positively in challenging situations, maintain your focus or stay in your performance zone, positive mental rehearsal will really help you improve in these areas. It will also improve your confidence in situations where you are experiencing something for the first time, e.g. your first international event, because you will be able to convince your brain that you have already performed in those conditions in advance of the competition. We always feel less confident when faced with a situation for the first time and after that initial test, we start to feel increasingly comfortable. Positive mental rehearsal can help deal with those 'first time' moments and create a more positive experience.

Just as negative mental rehearsal can produce the very scenario you were dreading, positive mental rehearsal can produce the performance outcome you want! In the same way that negative mental rehearsal is reinforced by negative experiences, creating a vicious circle, positive mental rehearsal allows you to create a virtuous circle.

This means when you vividly imagine riding well in a challenging situation (e.g. a competition or the first training event with a young horse), your brain can then make it a reality so you can feel more confident. This reinforces the images and movies in your mind and means you continue to practise this positive mental rehearsal. I recommend you practice on a daily basis over a three to four week period. Repetition is the key to success.

Here are the main benefits of using positive mental rehearsal to improve your performance level and consistency:

- ■ Improves your skills
- ■ Enables you to plan ahead to deal with a particular challenge
- ■ Allows you to take greater control over your emotions
- ■ Builds your confidence

TOP TIPS

Here are my top tips to get the best from positive mental rehearsal:

- Engage all your senses in creating a series of images or a movie so you really experience the scenario you are rehearsing.

- Make the images or movie very clear and bright.

- Focus on rehearsing one aspect of your performance, e.g. preparation and execution of right to left flying change, approach to and jumping of a specific fence.

- Make sure you're relaxed when you practise. A relaxed mind is a receptive mind!

- Practise it frequently to embed the positive experience, learning and improve your performance. The more familiar you are with the scenario and what you are doing it, the more able you will be to recreate that experience in your riding, whether you are at a competition, training event, schooling at home or on a hack.

ACTION

Make a list of all of the scenarios your regularly think about, either through imagining a picture, movie or through storytelling (i.e. an internal narrative). Now review each one and tick it if it has a positive effect on your riding performance and a cross if it has a negative effect.

Now review the list of negative mental rehearsal scenarios and work out which one occurs most frequently. This is your priority scenario to focus on and, at this stage, you need to put the other negative mental rehearsal scenarios to one side and return to them after you have successfully dealt with the priority scenario.

Next, work out what alternative scenario you could rehearse that would enable you to produce a positive outcome. Focus on how you can take positive action when you ride e.g. shoulders back, leg on. Focusing on what you can control is key. Now create a series of images or a movie in your mind of this new positive scenario. Make sure you see yourself and your horse in these images/movie and make it big and bright. See how you are riding, what you are doing and how your horse is responding.

For example, if you imagine riding towards a cross-country fence and your horse stops, imagine instead that you are riding positively before the fence and getting the right rhythm, then see yourself and your horse clearing the fence.

Focus on practising one thing at a time and keep it really simple. This is about creating new positive outcomes, and that can only happen when you are calm and focused.

If you compete, I recommend you create this scenario in your ridden practise at home before the competition so that your positive mental rehearsal and your practical ridden practise are aligned. This will allow you to continually reinforce the positive scenario using real and imagined experience.

I recommend that you mentally rehearse your new positive scenario three times every day for three to four weeks. By doing this regularly you will be more able to turn your imagined experience into reality each time you ride.

Remember that to get different results you need to take different actions, so by doing this practise every day, you will be more able to achieve better results.

TRANSFORM YOUR INNER CRITIC INTO YOUR BEST SUPPORTER

Maintaining a positive attitude is absolutely essential to being able to deal with the highs and lows of riding and competing. If you struggle to maintain a positive attitude, it's useful to understand the source of the problem, and one of the main ways to do this is to start tuning in to your internal dialogue. We talk to ourselves all the time, whether we are aware of it or not. If your internal dialogue is positive, you will focus on the positives in any given situation. If, however, you indulge in negative thinking, you will not focus on the positives and only see, hear and feel negatives.

It's important that you consistently choose where to place your focus because wherever your focus goes your energy follows. So if you focus on talking to yourself negatively, your attention on what's happening in your external environment also turns towards the negative aspects. What that means is that when you ride, your focus is likely to shift to the things you cannot control rather than the things you can control. What that also means is you have less control over your riding performance. So making sure that your inner critic is well under control is a key mindset strategy that will enable you to improve your riding performance, simply by maintaining your focus on positive actions you can take in challenging situations, whether you are competing, at a training event or taking a young horse on their first solo hack.

STORY-TELLING

Once you tune in to your inner voice and listen to what it is saying, you will notice that your inner voice is in the business of story-telling. In fact, we tell ourselves stories all the time. We commentate on everything from our interpretations of particular situations, to how we think we are doing. In telling ourselves these stories, we either support ourselves or we beat ourselves up. Often we talk more harshly to ourselves than we would with other people, and for some of the riders I work with, their inner voice occasionally becomes externally expressed, affecting their relationship with the people who support them.

The type of story we tell ourselves often depends on the situation we find ourselves in. For most riders, their inner voice tends to be positive when they are not in a pressurised situation and becomes negative when they are under pressure or dealing with a challenging situation.

Just like when we read a story in a book or see a story being played out on screen, our internal story-telling can evoke powerful emotions, particularly if we feel anxious, nervous or stressed. This means your inner voice is able to trigger positive or negative emotions depending on the story you tell yourself. When it is positive, it has the power to make you feel confident and in control, which allows you to ride positively and make quick, effective decisions. When it is negative, it can be incredibly destructive. When we talk negatively to ourselves, we are effectively telling ourselves stories. Just like a horror film, these stories conjure up scary pictures and feelings that impact on our energy, motivation and confidence. This is particularly damaging when you are competing because it causes you to doubt yourself, often resulting in overthinking and defensive riding.

Some riders believe that a negative inner voice is necessary for achieving their goals because they believe their inner critic keeps them focused on what they need to improve and prevents them from becoming over-confident. However, the reality is that a critical inner voice does far more damage than good. I have worked with riders whose inner critic is so loud and so demeaning that they freeze at competitions, unable to make decisions and perform because their inner

the key to overcoming your inner critic is to consciously notice it and challenge it a number of times, so you can break the habit and make a new, more positive one. Remember that as soon as your stress level increases and you notice feelings of anxiety, nerves or tension, your inner critic gets stronger and has more power. So you will find it much easier to challenge and deal with your inner critic when you are away from stressful riding situations because you will be more calm and able to control your thoughts. If you compete, then you should work on managing your internal dialogue away from the competition environment because this is a naturally challenging situation and causes an increase in stress.

Here are three simple steps to switching off autopilot and transforming your inner critic into your best supporter:

Step 1: Tune in to your inner critic – notice your thoughts and pay attention to the words being used. Notice how that makes you feel and where you feel it in your body. Notice if the words are following a pattern or continuous loop. Write down the key phrases that make you feel anxious, nervous or stressed.

Step 2: Challenge your inner critic – imagine that your best friend or your best supporter is with you right now. What would they be saying to the inner critic? How would they be challenging your critic? What exact words would they be using? How do these words and phrases make you feel? Write these words and phrases down in a notebook or make a note of them in your phone. These words need to be somewhere that you can easily access when your inner critic starts to take control. Memorise at least one of those positive phrases so that you can use this when you are riding.

Step 3: Interrupt and replace – there are lots of ways to interrupt your inner critic and my favourite ways are to say "stop" (either out loud or in your head), pinch yourself (if you are riding do this on the back of your hand), or take a very long deep breath and notice the cool air going in through your nose as you breathe in and warm air going out of your nose as you breathe out. Once you've interrupted your inner critic, replace the negative noise with 1-2 positive supportive phrases that you noted down in step 2. Notice the effect that it has on how you feel and how you ride. You may need to experiment with positive phrases to find the one that has the most positive effect. Remember this is about regaining balance and perspective.

If you are having a bad day, remember that one bad day is just that and nothing more. Just as you have had great days in the past, you will have those days again. Sometimes bad luck just happens and, when it does, it is tempting to think that you are destined to encounter more bad luck. Be determined to create your own luck, and by taking control of your inner critic you will be much more empowered to do just that!

ACTION

Complete steps 1 to 3 in the Switch Off Autopilot section. If you believe your inner critic helps you or if you unclear about whether your inner dialogue is negative or positive , ask yourself "How does this help me ride at my best?" This will help to clarify the impact of your inner critic and help you understand how it holds you back from riding at your best.

When you tune in to your inner critic in step 1, check your energy level and consider if it is sufficient for you to ride at your best. Remember that your inner critic will lower your energy levels by progressively destroying your motivation and confidence. Think about how your inner critic affects your energy levels and score yourself on an energy scale of 1 to 10 where 1 is no energy at all and 10 is fired up and ready to go!

In steps 2 and 3, think about the words and phrases you will use to tap into your best supporter and bring your realist voice to the front and centre of your mind. Consider how this affects your energy levels and score yourself again on a scale of 1 to 10 where 1 is no energy at all and 10 is fired up and ready to go!

DEALING WITH SETBACKS

Your inner critic loves setbacks. It thrives when you make mistakes, have a bad day or if your carefully constructed plan doesn't work out. It waits until you are at your lowest ebb and then it pounces and attacks. This means that when you experience a setback, it is important to be alert to the danger of your inner critic resurfacing. Perhaps you feel you were marked unfairly in your dressage test or you had a stop cross-country, or you had a pole down in the showjumping, or maybe your training session didn't go to plan. Whatever the challenge, you need to regroup quickly and, to do this, you need your inner voice to take the realist position.

It's normal to have a moment of frustration and to experience that feeling. What isn't OK is to beat yourself up because that will damage your confidence and self-belief. When you do this, your inner critic wins and you lose.

To get your inner voice to switch to the realist position, remind yourself of all the things you do well when you ride. This will help you regain perspective. Then reflect on what you have learnt from experiencing the setback and what you will improve next time. Doing this automatically turns a negative into a positive.

It is important to practise and get good at accessing your inner realist as quickly as possible. To help you do this, use the key words and phrases your best supporter would say to you to quieten your inner critic so you can refocus on the positives.

You can use the same three simple steps I outlined earlier in this chapter to help you. I cannot emphasise enough how important it is that you master this mindset skill. If you simply beat yourself up, all you're doing is stripping your self-confidence and resilience, and it isn't going to help you perform well (remember the blindfold experiment I mentioned earlier).

CHAMPION YOURSELF

It's part of our culture in the UK that we think it is boastful to celebrate our successes. Many of us downplay our successes or we congratulate the fact that the horse made a massive effort, with the intention of being modest, when in fact it detracts from our own success. Riders do this partly because of their mindset but partly because our culture dictates that we should do that.

When you fail to acknowledge these things, your inner critic starts to gain power, so take time out to celebrate your successes and acknowledge what you have achieved. This will boost your confidence and improve your skill in interrupting and quietening your inner critic. In short, it will get you better connected with your best supporter and the realist position that you want your inner voice to take.

Doing this means you will have the energy and focus needed to build confidence, ride at your best under pressure and bounce back from setbacks more quickly. It means when the going gets tough, you get going! Ultimately this will set you up for success and make it much more likely that you will achieve your goals.

MASTER YOUR EMOTIONS

Emotional control is absolutely essential to enable you to perform at your best under pressure. The part of your brain that controls emotions is separate from the intelligent, supercomputer part that makes quick, accurate decisions and allows you to apply all of your skills and experience to a situation. The super-computer part of your brain is called the pre-frontal cortex and it is extremely demanding. In order for it to work effectively it needs a lot of energy, and so if the emotional centre in your brain is very active, it consumes so much energy that the prefrontal cortex cannot work effectively.

Therefore, being able to control your emotions isn't simply a psychological technique, it's a biological and mechanical imperative. The bottom line is that you will not be able to ride well if you are experiencing highly intense emotions.

For some riders, just knowing this fact is helpful because they get stuck in a vicious cycle of getting anxious, nervous or stressed, so they are more tense when they ride, which means they don't ride at their best, then beat themselves up for not riding well. This makes the feelings of anxiety, nerves and stress more intense and so the vicious cycle continues. When you understand that to perform better you need to reduce the intensity of the emotion you are feeling and you take action to make this happen, you will instantly improve how you ride.

Just like pressure, emotions are a form of energy and so they are not things you can simply remove from your riding experience. So it's not about eliminating emotions, it's about reducing them and controlling them at a level that enables you to direct your mental energy to your pre-frontal cortex.

Throughout this chapter, I'm going to be explaining exactly how to master your emotions and, rather than going into a lot of technical detail about the brain, I'm simply going to show you how to gain greater control over your emotions and activate your pre-frontal cortex. This entire chapter is really all about allowing your pre-frontal cortex to work because whilst it is the best piece of technology you own (yes, really), it is extremely demanding and unless it has the right conditions, it will not function optimally. Think of your prefrontal cortex like a diva. You need to meet its demands first before it will perform for you!

NOT ALL EMOTIONS ARE CREATED EQUAL

The world's top riders are able to exert such control over their emotions that they are able to stay in an optimal state that enables them to ride at their best. They are able to access emotions that empower them, whilst minimising the impact of negative emotions like stress, tension and nerves.

So whilst it is essential that you feel psyched up, motivated and ready to ride, if this becomes stress, nerves or any other negative emotion, you start to lose control and your emotions start to control you. In contrast, positive emotions enable you to take control of the situation and prepare you to perform at your best. This is a key part of how riders can transform pressure into power, by identifying and replacing negative emotions with positive, empowering ones.

When negative emotions take control and overpower you, it is common to experience 'choking.' This is a phenomenon observed in all sports where the participant becomes so anxious, nervous or stressed that they start to over-analyse and overthink, which means their energy is invested in the wrong place and leaves no capacity for them to execute their skills effectively. This means that they underperform even though they are capable of producing a much better performance. This happens to a lot of riders I work with, who become so anxious about a challenging situation, like jumping a clear showjumping round, that they overthink the striding and approach to the jumps and end up having poles down. To avoid 'choking' you must learn to master your emotions.

EARLY WARNING SIGNS

The first and most essential step for mastering your emotions is learning how to recognise the early warning signs. In an earlier chapter I outlined the importance of identifying the early warning signs of pressure, and since pressure and emotions are interconnected, it is vital that you intercept negative emotions before they overwhelm you. Pressure and emotions have a driving effect on each other – when one increases so does the other. However, when you are able to take control you can reduce the pressure you experience by reducing the intensity of your emotions.

Becoming skilled at mastering your emotions is all about being able to identify and intercept the early warning signs, because this is when the emotions are at a relatively low intensity and it's easier to control them. If you wait until the intensity has built and you feel overwhelmed, you'll find it much more difficult to regain control because you'll have used up a lot of mental energy by that stage.

Here are some of the early warning signs you need to look out for:

- Feeling worried, nervous, anxious, tense or stressed
- Headache, loss of appetite, tired or lethargic
- Poor quality and/or quantity of sleep
- Drop in motivation level
- Negative thoughts
- Self-doubt
- Feeling compelled to double-check everything
- Focusing on worst case or what-if scenarios

These are very common early warning signs that I encounter in my work with riders. When you are able to recognise and deal with the early warning signs you will instantly gain more control over how you ride under pressure and in challenging situations.

ACTION

Think about the last time you felt negative emotions overwhelming you and make a note of the situation and the emotions you were feeling in that situation. Labelling the emotions helps you identify the source of the problem. For example, nerves are often a sign that you lack confidence or self belief. Next, think about what was happening before you felt overwhelmed and identify the early warning signs. Think about what triggers these early warning signs – is it a negative belief, your inner critic or worrying about what could go wrong?

IDENTIFY, INTERRUPT, REPLACE, REPEAT

Once you've started to identify your early warning signs and have more insight into what triggers negative emotions, the next step is to identify it when it happens, interrupt it and replace the emotion with something else.

Remember that emotions are energy and you cannot destroy energy; you can only change it and transform it into something else. It's about making a mindset shift from being in a right state to being in the right state.

Interrupting the negative emotion means that you stop it in its tracks and prevent it from escalating and controlling you. Riders often find that relaxation techniques are very effective in interrupting negative emotions. Taking action to prevent negative emotions escalating will enable you to take back control and ride more positively in challenging situations. When you consistently interrupt negative emotions and take back control, it will help you to ride better and perform more consistently whether you are riding at competition, in a training event, schooling or hacking.

By consistently interrupting negative emotions regularly and replacing it with a more empowering emotion like confidence, you will break the association between being in a challenging situation and feeling the negative emotion like stress, nerves or anxiety. At the same time, you'll also build a new association between riding in a challenging situation and feeling confident. Once this new association is established, you will have achieved a shift in your mindset by creating a new, empowering habit that helps you to ride at your best.

For example, let's say that you currently feel worried every time you start walking the showjumping course, which results in you focusing on the fences that you think your horse may spook at. If it is something that happens every time, you may not even be aware of it because it's an automatic response that your brain produces each time you walk a course. Your brain has learnt to associate walking the course with feeling worried and tense. By interrupting this emotion and replacing it with calm confidence every time you walk a showjumping course, over time you will break down this habit of worrying and instead you will simply feel calm and confident when you walk a course.

Interrupting a negative emotion can be as simple as taking a slow deep breath and just acknowledging what is happening. You may find it useful to say "stop" either in your head or out loud as an interruption strategy.

To replace the negative emotion you are experiencing, use a relaxation technique to reduce the intensity of the negative emotion and then choose an alternative, positive emotion.

It could be confident, happy, excited, motivated, calm. Simply choose an emotion and then remember a recent time when you felt that emotion.

Focus on what you saw, heard and felt. Remember where you felt that emotion in your body. Then ask yourself, "what can I do to feel that way when I ride?" Connecting with a positive emotion will help you to redirect your mental energy to the part of your brain that needs to work well for you to ride at your best.

Then simply repeat as often as possible to embed a new empowering emotional habit. By practising this process you will not only establish a more useful habit that enables your brain to function well, you will also build your skill in mastering your emotions.

The reason this mindset strategy has such a powerful positive effect is because most of the time, you are unlikely to be aware of your emotional habits, and so because you are not aware of them, you also do not challenge them. This means that habits that hinder your riding performance simply get repeated over and over again automatically, and over time this simply serves to reinforce and strengthen the habit. Once you recognise these negative emotional habits, interrupt them and replace them with a more positive, empowering emotion, then you can start to form a habit that will enable you to ride at your best.

The more you practise, the more able you will be to embed the new empowering emotional habit. I work with some riders every week for one month to help them achieve this, because research shows it takes 30 days of consistent practise to embed a new habit.

Negative emotional habits can also be created by your belief system and your inner critic, so it's important to examine your beliefs and inner critic (refer to the chapters earlier in this book) and challenge those to help you overcome negative emotional habits.

ACTION

Identify a relaxation technique you can use to reduce the intensity of the negative emotions you experience. Then select a positive emotion that you will use to replace negative emotions and commit to implementing the identify-interrupt-replace-repeat process I've described every day for 30 days.

STRESS TEST

Emotional mastery is not just about being able to control your emotions; it's about being able to quickly connect with your optimal emotional state for performance. You may remember I mentioned that the pre-frontal cortex is demanding. Well, it has a very specific set of demands. In order to work at it's very best, it needs energy in the form of oxygen and blood flow, and lots of it! Unless you are in an optimal emotional and physical state, your pre-frontal cortex will not get enough oxygen, protein and glucose and so it will not be able to function at its best. So you need to be in an optimal emotional state to enable your brain to perform optimally.

When you are in an optimal emotional state, you will be motivated, psyched up and ready to go. You will experience pressure and a degree of stress, but you will be using this to get prepared and ready to ride. You will be able to use this stress to focus on the task in hand, whether it's competing, a training event, schooling or hacking. Everyone needs a different level of stress to be in this optimal emotional state and so it is important that you identify the exact level of stress you need to ride at your best.

Your optimal emotional state is what allows you to get focused and access your performance zone. Without your optimal emotional state you will not be able to get into and stay in your zone because the part of your brain that enables you to be in your performance zone is, yes you've guessed it, your prefrontal cortex!

ACTION

Think back to the last time you rode at your best and think about how you felt. What thoughts were going through your mind? What was your focus and concentration like? How would you describe your emotions? What was your posture like? Write down the answers to these questions and use it as a guide to help you access your performance zone. Practise getting into this optimal emotional state each time you ride, when there is no pressure, so that you are more able to get into this optimal emotional state when it matters most.

EMOTIONAL SCALES

One of the reasons riders have coaching sessions with me is that they find it difficult to manage their emotional scales. They find that excitement turns into nerves and motivation becomes anxiety. Managing your emotional scales is important because it helps you to also manage your energy levels. I think of emotions as being on a scale where the positive emotion is on the left and requires less mental energy, and on the right you have the negative emotion that requires more energy, like this:

Low energy drain	High energy drain
Motivated	Anxious

Where are you on this scale when you ride or compete? Are you closer to the motivated or anxious end? How does that affect your thoughts, feelings and how you ride?

Remember that when you feel intense negative emotions that your pre-frontal cortex, the part of your brain responsible for making decisions and enabling you to use your riding skills cannot work properly, which prevents you from riding to the best of your ability. We have a price to pay for the very sophisticated technology that we have in the pre-frontal cortex and that price is mental energy. Because our pre-frontal cortex burns through energy really quickly (if it was a car it would be a sports car!) you have to be really careful about how you use your mental energy. This is why mastering your emotions is a really powerful mindset strategy. It also explains why we find it difficult to take back control when we feel intense negative emotions. It is the pre-frontal cortex that helps you take back control of your emotions and that is why recognising and interrupting the early warning signs is so important.

Understanding where you are on your emotional scale and managing your emotional state is critical, because positive emotions can quickly become negative and overwhelm you when you are under pressure, which means you can quickly lose control of your emotions and your pre-frontal cortex is unable to work properly. When you allow your emotions and the pressure of a challenging situation to control you, you lose your ability to think and ride positively. That also means that your horse is likely to become uncertain about what you want and may become more hesitant or distracted.

To really master your emotions, you must be prepared to switch off autopilot mode and complete the exercises I've outlined in this chapter. You need to increase your self-awareness to catch negative emotions early before they become overwhelming. It sounds simple and it is; be aware though that it's also hard work. It is possible to make significant improvements to your mindset, confidence and focus so it's worthwhile investing time and effort.

TROUBLESHOOTING

This section outlines a few of the most common problems that competition riders I work with are experiencing, and my suggested solutions.

Creeping, crippling nerves

Many riders I work with don't know they are nervous until they are struck by an attack of nerves. Experiencing nerves is normal but it's about having control over them that makes a difference between staying calm under pressure and becoming overwhelmed. The solution to this lies in the Identify-Interrupt-Replace-Repeat process I described earlier in this chapter. Follow that process and you will soon find that nerves no longer creep up on you!

Fear of failure

Even when you have a high level of motivation and commitment to achieve your goals, fear of failure can really hold you back. Fear of failure is most intense when the outcome you want to achieve is very important to you. Achieving your goal then becomes a pass/fail test which increases the pressure you experience. Overcoming fear of failure makes all the difference to your ability to ride at your best. To illustrate this, let's imagine we're looking at the mindset of two riders, both of whom are highly motivated to achieve a win at competition.

Rider A has a low fear of failure. This means that Rider A approaches every competition full of energy, even if the conditions are not great and the outcome is very uncertain. Rider A will take calculated risks and will be incredibly determined and resilient to overcome setbacks and keep going to achieve their ultimate goal.

Rider B has a high fear of failure. This means that whilst Rider B takes personal responsibility for their outcomes, mistakes, problems and setbacks cause self-doubt and damage self-confidence. Rider B worries about failing a lot, which means they're less likely to be able to move past setbacks and less persistent in continuing to work towards achieving their ultimate goal. This means that Rider B is very unlikely to fulfil their potential.

Where's your motivation coming from? Is it coming from an internal source, e.g. a sense of achievement, or is it coming from an external source, e.g. desire for external recognition, sponsorship, awards, rosettes, titles? Once you understand your motivation, you need to make sure you set goals that focus on the job you need to do as a rider to give you the best possible chance of achieving the results you want. For example, if you get tense when you compete, focusing on relaxation and making that your goal will help you ride more effectively and produce a better performance than focusing on achieving a result – a particular dressage score, jumping clear, a placing or win. This will enable you to focus on achieving things that you can control and help you to realize that you have more control over your riding performance than you thought.

Feeling emotionally drained and fatigued

This happens when riders do not conserve their mental energy. Remember that riding is a high mental skill sport; it is an endurance test for your brain and you need to conserve energy. Relaxation does a number of things: it lowers your heart rate, it lowers your blood pressure and it also allows you to conserve your energy. Focus on relaxation techniques to help you slow your thinking and reduce stress. Thinking too fast will result in fatigue. Remember that the only thing you can control is what's happening in the present moment, so just focus on the here and now and take some time, even if it's just a few minutes, to relax. There are a variety of different relaxation techniques you can use. Try relaxing the muscles in your arms in your legs and take a few deep breaths, then relax the muscles in your face and neck. This will bring your focus into the present moment, quieten your mind and help you think about what you need to be doing right now in order to set yourself up for success. When you conserve energy in this way, it means you have greater mental energy to make quick decisions.

Unable to let go of setbacks

Many riders struggle to let go of setbacks they have experienced or mistakes they have made, especially at competition, and will often beat themselves up for some time after the setback has occurred. Their thoughts will often have a pattern or repetitive loop to them. Being stuck in a negative pattern or loop of thinking will impact your confidence and create more negative thinking. If you experience this, it's important to interrupt your inner critic as it is usually your inner voice that is responsible for creating these negative thought patterns and loops. Remember our inner critic is strongest when we are feeling stressed, tense, nervous, frustrated, angry or disappointed. It thrives on negative emotions. Take a step back and reflect on what you can learn from the setback and what you can improve next time. There is always another day and opportunity to ride well and perform at your best. You can only control what happens in the here and now. By doing that you will be more able to influence the future. You certainly will not be able to change what has happened in the past. Remember that when you believe that failures and errors are a sign that you won't ever succeed and achieve your goals, it's inevitable that you'll feel disappointed and frustrated. However, it's only when you give up that you truly fail. Everything else is a source of valuable feedback and an opportunity to learn, so you can improve and progress. When you experience a setback, ask yourself, "How could I use this to improve my performance next time?" By focusing your attention on what you have learnt you set yourself up for future success.

Feeling demotivated after a setback

The best antidote to this is to make sure you celebrate your successes when they happen. No matter how small the success, make sure you take time to acknowledge it to yourself and enjoy the moment! Celebrating successes is critical for confidence, self-belief and motivation. If you don't celebrate your successes, you can lose perspective and stop noticing positives, which means you lose motivation to keep going when the going gets tough. Make sure you acknowledge when things go well by writing your successes in a journal so you can remind yourself of previous successes when you encounter a setback. Even when you experience a setback, reflect on what went well because something will have gone well; it's just that we lose sight of this when we're disappointed and frustrated. Acknowledge what has gone well so that you gain a more balanced perspective of the situation. It's important to acknowledge both the positives and negatives of situations to create a more balanced view of situations which will help you build confidence, learn from setbacks and progress towards achieving your goals.

HOW TO DEVELOP POSITIVE FOCUS

The ability to ride at your best is determined by both your technical riding skills and focus. Focus is often overlooked as a valuable mindset skill, particularly in an era where technology divides our focus and decreases our attention span. We value multitasking over having a single point of focus. However, when you are riding and competing, your ability to concentrate and focus positively on the task at hand is crucial. Developing positive focus is about improving the length of time that you can focus for (focal endurance) and consistently directing your focus on to the factors that you can control (focal control) so that you can take positive action. When you develop positive focus, you will be able to access your performance zone exactly when you need it in challenging situations. Positive focus is what helps you stay in your performance zone and protects you against distractions. It's like a protective bubble where the only things you notice are you, your horse and the task, e.g. jumping, dressage, schooling.

Whilst there may still be occasions when you get distracted, because sometimes there are unavoidable distractions (e.g. a loose dog on a cross country course), positive focus enables you to refocus and get back into your performance zone within a few seconds rather than taking minutes to refocus or maybe not refocusing at all!

Positive focus allows you to make quick decisions and adjustments so that you are more able to deal with whatever happens when you ride and compete. You'll be able to think more clearly because your mind will be quieter and you'll be able to focus entirely on the task at hand. Positive focus is a fundamental feature of your performance zone.

Being able to control and direct your focus is critical for confidence and performance because it will enable you to ride positively under pressure. Your focus is like a mental spotlight. Whatever you focus on is what you see and experience, whilst everything else is cast into shadow. When you change your focus, you change what you see, hear and feel. It gives you an entirely new perspective on a situation. When you consistently direct your focus on to taking positive action, you will be more able to ride at your best.

KNOW YOUR TARGET

Without motivation and clarity on what you want to achieve, it can be difficult to maintain positive focus. In the absence of clear goals, riders often focus on what they don't want, which has a negative effect on their confidence and motivation. Maintaining positive focus is energy intense, so you have to be really motivated to maintain it so you focus on the task at hand, rather than judging and assessing how you're riding.

The first step to developing positive focus is to know what you want to achieve from each competition, training session or schooling session. Remember to focus on how you want to ride and what you can do to achieve the result you desire. By focusing on this, you increase your chance of success because you can exert more control over how you ride.

GET THE RIGHT QUALITY

The recent digital age of technology means we are increasingly being asked to divide our attention between multiple tasks. The conscious mind is ineffective at dividing attention between multiple tasks and, whilst technology perhaps makes it a little easier for us to do this, it's not a strategy that works when you ride.

Our conscious mind can only really focus with accuracy and quality on one thing at a time, and when we ask it to do more than this the quality of our focus decreases. When that happens in a riding situation, your conscious mind is likely to become overloaded and this is quite often what will trigger an increase in anxiety, stress, tension or nerves. You can start to worry or doubt yourself or get stressed by the number of things that you're trying to focus on. Your brain goes into overdrive and this is when you start to overthink, overanalyse and override.

So if you do a lot of multi-tasking, it's important to rethink this when you ride. It can be difficult to develop positive focus if you're used to getting distracted regularly on a day-to-day basis. However, when you ride it is absolutely essential that you are 100% focused on the task at hand, whether it's riding a dressage test, negotiating a ditch or jumping a double. When you give something 100% attention to the exclusion of everything else going on around you, you are positively focused! Positive focus is absolutely essential for helping you to stay in your performance zone. Without it, you will find yourself getting distracted very quickly.

Often riders will analyse all the things that need to go well to achieve their goal. If you try to focus on all of these things at once, two things will happen. First you feel overwhelmed by the level of challenge in front of you. It is a bit like wanting to climb Everest and all the way up simply staring at the top. If you did that you would soon lose focus on putting one foot in front of the other and getting to the top. Second, you try to focus on too many things and that is when your brain starts to overanalyze, rather than allowing things to flow and just taking one thing at a time. Developing positive focus is all about your ability to focus on one thing at a time.

So to develop positive focus, you first need to make sure that you are completely immersed in the task at hand, so you can remain focused in the present moment. Secondly, you need to focus on one thing at a time. It sounds simple, doesn't it? Although it's simple, it's not easy, and that is why it is a skill you can develop over time.

CHOOSE YOUR DIRECTION

Positive focus is not just about length of focus (focal endurance), it's about direction (focal control). If you direct your focus on to something you cannot control, you will find it difficult to stay in your performance zone. To stay in your performance zone you need to be focused on what you can control and nothing else. That means distractions, your inner critic, anxious thoughts and thinking about the result you could achieve, all needs to be put to one side. These things lead you down a path of focusing on things you cannot control. So it's important to take steps to improve the direction of your focus so you stay in your performance zone.

Many riders I work with become fixated on outcomes, e.g. competition results. This is a distraction in itself because when you focus on an outcome you think about the future rather than staying grounded in the present moment and focused on the task in hand. Other riders reflect on previous experiences, focusing on times when they haven't ridden well, something has gone wrong or they haven't achieved the result they want, which means that they think about the past, rather than focusing on what is happening in the present moment.

Whilst it's tempting to time travel to the past or the future when you're riding, it's essential you stay focused on the present moment. When you do this, it means that, if something doesn't go to plan, you can adjust your riding and remain positively focused despite the challenge.

ACTION

To improve your positive focus, it's important to first examine what triggers negative focus. Make a list of all the negative thoughts you have that relate to: a) factors you cannot control, b) 'what if' scenarios, c) things you don't want to happen (e.g. "don't get tense," "don't panic," "don't mess it up"). Then consider what it is that you want to achieve, identify what you can control that will help you achieve the outcome you want, then create two to three commands that will help you to ride more effectively, e.g. ride positively, let go, soft hands, sit tall. Then practice using these commands when you ride to help you create more positive focus.

Next, make a list of all the things that tend to distract you when you are riding. Then look at each one in turn and work out how you could adjust your focus so you can take positive action instead to focus on the task in hand. You'll find it helpful to consider what you need to do in order to ride well, e.g. get the horse listening to you, leg on, accurate transitions. You can then use mental rehearsal (see earlier chapter) to help you prepare to deal with the distraction. Often we react to distractions out of habit so it's important to take action to break that habit.

PRACTISE PRODUCES FOCUS

Remember that positive focus is a skill that you need to develop and so it's important to practise.

I recommend you complete the action in this chapter and then practise achieving the right quality and direction of focus each time you ride. Initially practice it in situations where there is little or no pressure and challenge. It is important to practise positive focus in these situations because it will help you make improvements. Remember that a challenging situation will put your positive focus to the test, so if you haven't established positive focus in situations where there is little or no pressure, you will find it difficult to maintain positive focus when you are under pressure.

When you are practising this skill, make sure you are breathing and have eaten a snack two hours before riding. If at any point during your practise you are not breathing deeply enough, there will not be enough flow of oxygen going to your brain to maintain positive focus. Fueling your brain is a fundamental requirement for positive focus.

Because positive focus is more mentally demanding and intense, you may not be able to sustain it for very long at first. Positive focus is like a muscle – you need to build strength and endurance over time. You can measure how strong it is by setting a stopwatch and timing yourself whilst riding, to see how long you can sustain positive focus when you are in low pressure situations and high pressure situations. You may find that the length of time you can maintain positive focus varies according to the situation. It's important to measure it so you can establish a baseline. Once you have completed the action in this chapter and completed 2-3 weeks of positive focus practice, measure it again and see what the difference is in the length of time you can maintain your positive focus. You will find that your ability to control the direction of your focus and the length of time that you can maintain positive focus improves with practice.

The maximum amount of time you should be aiming for is 20 minutes as it is extremely difficult to sustain positive focus for much longer than this because of how energy intense this mental skill is. You should plan for a natural distraction break after 20 minutes. This break should be around 3-10 seconds, then refocus. Your internal 'focus timer' will then reset and you should be able to focus for another 20 minutes.

RITUALS & ROUTINES TO BOOST YOUR PERFORMANCE

Rituals and routines are key mindset tools that enable you to switch yourself into performance mode and get into your zone. You may have noticed that professional sports people have routines that they always go through before and during competitions. Often these routines are labelled as 'superstitions,' which makes them seem like they are frivolous and irrelevant, but they are actually the key to helping the athlete or sports person unlock their performance potential.

The reason routines are labelled as 'superstitions' is because they have meaning to the person using them but they may have no logical or rational meaning to other people. You can argue that triggers, which I cover in the next chapter, fall into the same category. It doesn't matter if the routine, ritual or trigger makes logical sense or not; it just needs to help the person perform at their best. If it serves that purpose, that is what matters.

Obviously in equestrian sport, there is the horse to consider and so any routine, ritual or trigger must be safe for the horse and rider, and it must also not compromise the horse's ability to perform. So for example, a warm-up routine must effectively warm up the horse to prepare it for the athletic challenge ahead and prevent injury, whilst also helping the rider to get focused and in their performance zone.

In this chapter, I'm going to outline some of the most common rituals and routines that can help riders deal with pressure more effectively. These are repeatable processes that you can use as often as you need to when you are riding and competing.

EFFECTIVE ROUTINES & RITUALS

Effective routines and rituals give you certainty, control and a plan of action. You can find examples of routines and rituals in everyday life as well as in sports, because they make us feel safe to take on challenging situations. Routines and rituals are effective not because of the actions per se, but because they create a positive and confident state of mind. This helps us to deal with potentially stressful situations by reinforcing positive feelings and behaviours. Positive mental rehearsal (discussed in an earlier chapter) is just one example of a ritual that can create a strong sense of control, confidence and focus.

When you are riding under pressure, you will often be in a situation that is testing, uncertain and unpredictable, so having routines and rituals in place will give you reassurance and a greater sense of control. Routines and rituals also help you to focus so you can get in to your performance zone, helping you to conserve vital mental energy and control your emotions.

Here are some of the most effective rituals and routines that enable riders to respond positively in challenging situations.

Pre-competition

If you compete then this routine will help you to prepare before competitions and focus your attention on the upcoming competition. This type of routine covers everything from the last work session you do with your horse before a competition, to the process of packing your lorry or trailer. It is common for riders to have a series of these pre-competition routines that they carry out in the final week before each competition. This is a routine that I will explain in further detail later on in this chapter.

Warm-up

Having a warm-up routine is good for you and it's good for your horse, particularly if you ride young or inexperienced horses. Routine gives horses comfort in the uncertain and unpredictable environment. It has the same benefit for you and, because it gets you focused on riding each step of the routine, it enables you to get in to your performance zone so distractions such as people watching and busy warm-up areas become less intrusive and you can adjust your riding as required. The better you know the routine and the more precisely you ride it, the more effective the routine will be in a competition environment. So make sure you practise it at home and know it back to front!

Refocusing

Have a routine or ritual that allows you to refocus and get back in your performance zone quickly. This could be a deep breath, saying something to yourself or simply riding a shape like a 10m circle to give you time to refocus. This will help you to limit the impact that distractions have on your riding and help you refocus more quickly.

Mental rehearsal

As well as being a mindset strategy (see earlier chapter) mental rehearsal is also a routine that you can use to switch yourself into performance mode.

PRE-COMPETITION ROUTINES

If you compete then it's important to examine how you mentally prepare for competitions. Whether you're aware of it or not, you already have pre-competition routines and rituals; it's just that they may be unhelpful rather than being something that aids your riding performance.

One pre-competition ritual I have come across is something I call 'the wind-up.' Some riders use the time before a competition to get nervous and wound up about the challenges they may face. Clearly this will not help them on the day, as it builds up their stress levels in advance of the competition, which will only further intensify once the day of the competition arrives.

So it's important that you establish some clear pre-competition routines as well as competition day routines and rituals that help you manage your stress, conserve your mental energy and get you ready to switch into performance mode and into your zone.

Effective pre-competition routines are essential for getting you in the right state of mind to ride at your best and give you the best possible chance of achieving the outcome you want. These routines will give you a greater sense of control going into the competition and will help you and your horse to remain calm.

The best pre-competition routines are simple. Keeping it simple means your routine will be predictable and easy to repeat for every competition.

Write down everything you believe you need to do in order to prepare for the competition, including what exercise routine your horse needs to perform at his/her best. Being clear about the optimal plan for your horse is essential. This will depend on your horse's preferences and fitness. Only you will know what works for your horse; just make sure you have a clear plan that gets your horse prepared and ready to perform. Once you've completed your list, go through it and evaluate the importance of each item. Check that you have included the essential things like checking your horse's shoes, packing your equipment, food, first aid kit, etc.

Your pre-competition routine must include a deadline for finishing up practise. This is really important because last minute practise can negatively affect your competition performance if it doesn't go well, especially if you are struggling with something, like a section of your dressage test. It is much better to practise the things that you are finding difficult and could be the weakest link in your performance as far in advance of the competition as possible, because trying to fix that last minute will likely damage your confidence and not set you up for success.

The next element you need in your pre-competition routine is a routine for eating, sleeping and generally taking care of yourself. To make sure you have sufficient mental energy for the competition, it is very important that you rest and eat well in the week leading up to the competition. Your muscles also need to be well rested, which should be balanced with your riding preparation.

Your pre-competition routine needs to be designed to reduce your stress so that you are well prepared, rather than leaving things to the last minute. This means planning ahead and working methodically through a checklist to complete each step of competition preparation, e.g. plating up, loading equipment on to the lorry or trailer.

STRUCTURE IS YOUR FRIEND

I recommend you create a competition preparation checklist to help guide you through the competition so that if things start to get overwhelming, you can simply review your checklist and identify the exact action you need to complete next. This will help you focus and give you back control.

Be completely open with whoever comes with you to competitions, about what you need from them in order to remain calm and focused. Remember rituals and routines are all about giving you control and allowing you to remain calm under pressure, so make sure you're really honest with the people around you about what you need them to do for you so you can implement the rituals and routines you need to remain confident and focused throughout the competition.

DESIGN YOUR OWN

So now you know more about some of the most helpful routines and rituals that help riders stay confident and focused under pressure, it's important you understand how to design your own rituals and routines. This is something I help many riders with, so here are my top tips:

- Keep it simple! Simple routines are far more powerful than complex ones so make sure you keep it simple.

- Remember the aim of a routine is to help you stay organised and feel in control so you can focus your attention on your riding.

- Focus on creating a routine or ritual that enables you to feel confident, focused and in control. Remember that what works for other people might not work for you – find what works for you and stick with it!

- Make sure your routine or ritual enables you to stay focused on the task in hand so you can get into your performance zone. This will also help you to quieten your inner critic and maintain the right level of stress and pressure that enables you to thrive under pressure and ride at your best.

- Adapt competition rituals and routines for non-competition situations where you experience anxiety, nerves or stress to help you ride more confidently and positively. The principles of what you do at competition often work just as effectively in non-competition situations.

ACTION

Make a list of all the rituals and routines you use. Include all the unhelpful ones as well as the ones that help you ride at your best. Then create new routines and rituals, using the information and tips in this chapter, that you can implement to replace the unhelpful ones, so you can ride with more confidence and positive focus.

DEVELOP TRIGGERS TO UNLOCK YOUR PERFORMANCE POWER

This mindset strategy is really powerful once you have established a strong set of positive beliefs, positive focus and you have control over your inner critic. For triggers to be effective, it's important to have a good level of self-awareness, which each of the other mindset strategies in this book will help you build. It is also useful to have a good awareness of the routines and rituals that work well for you, as that will give you direction and insight to help you identify effective triggers.

Triggers differ from routines and rituals because they are much shorter interventions and are designed to instantly boost your confidence and positive focus.

Just as triggers can be powerful tools that unlock your riding performance power, many of the riders I work with also have negative triggers, and you may find that as you work through this chapter, you identify a number of negative triggers. If this happens, I recommend you read the chapters on beliefs, mental rehearsal, inner critic and master your emotions. Be aware that there are some negative triggers, such as the memory of a fall or bad experience, that may require professional intervention from a sports or rider psychology coach to remove them before positive triggers can be established.

UNDERSTANDING TRIGGERS

Triggers are a natural part of human behaviour, and over your lifetime you will acquire numerous triggers, many of which you may not be consciously aware of. When I talk about triggers in this chapter, I am describing a stimulus-response process; that is, your brain produces a behavioural response to a stimulus. In NLP, we call this 'anchoring' and I often use this with riders to help them develop new triggers. The process of establishing and using triggers has been studied for a long time in psychology and perhaps the most famous of all studies in this area is Pavlov's dogs. In this experiment, the dogs would salivate every time a bowl of food was produced. The researchers then presented the bowl of food again and at the same time rang a bell. They repeated this process over and over again. Then they rang the bell without presenting the food to the dogs and the dogs salivated. This experiment demonstrated that not only is it possible for the brain to form new associations, but those associations do not necessarily need to make logical sense. For instance, why would it be logical for a dog to salivate just at the sound of a bell? However, trained or learned behaviour does not necessarily follow a logical pattern, In this case, the dogs had learnt that the bell and the food had a connection and therefore their brains associated the sound of a bell with food and produced the same behavioural response (salivating) as if they had actually been presented with food.

This is why, when we observe the so called 'superstitions' of world class sports people, we may think that they make no logical sense but it's very likely that these superstitions are acting as triggers that enable them to feel confident under pressure and focus positively on the task in hand. It makes no logical sense to us because we do not see the association that the sports person is making between the 'superstition' and feeling confident or focused. These 'superstitions' are often either triggers (small movement that triggers a response) or a ritual (a series of steps with multiple triggers).

So as you read through this chapter, remember that every trigger you have has been created by your brain learning to associate a particular stimulus – a sight, sound, movement – with a behavioural response – excitement, nerves, anxiety.

The response part of the trigger can have one of three different effects: positive, negative or neutral. When I work with riders, I help them identify positive and negative responses first, then I focus on enhancing and strengthening the positive responses so that riders can use these when they need them the most, and I also help riders to remove negative triggers, which is a process that can happen quickly. The reason for this is that your brain makes associations between different things all the time and is constantly updating its database of causes and effects. This means that, depending on how deeply embedded the association is, you can break it pretty quickly and replace it with a new one. Neuro-linguistic programming (NLP) provides some great tools and techniques for achieving this, which is why I am a big advocate of using NLP techniques when I work with riders, alongside more traditional sports psychology techniques.

ACTION

Remember a recent time when you were riding or competing in a challenging situation and identify the positive and negative triggers. Notice changes in how you were feeling, the level of confidence you had, how positively focused you were and go back to a few moments before you noticed the change in how you were feeling to identify the trigger. You may not have been aware of all of them so just remember as much as you can about moments where you noticed a change in how you felt and how you were riding. For example, some of the event riders I work with have a trigger at the point that they move from the showjumping warm-up to the arena. The point at which they move forward into the arena triggers a feeling of nerves or anxiety. This is just one example of a negative trigger. You will probably have examples of both positive and negative triggers so just think through what those are and make a list. Then look down your list and highlight the positive ones.

Make a new list of the positive ones and read it regularly to remind yourself of the triggers you can use to help you feel confident, focused and in control.

It is important to note that positive triggers are most effective when you use them occasionally. If you use them too often they start to lose their effect. This means that sometimes you may be able to overcome negative triggers by repeatedly exposing yourself to them until you learn that there is no negative consequence. There's a reason I have used the word 'sometimes.' It is relatively straightforward enough if it's something relatively low risk like public speaking. Let's say that you got nervous every time you stood up in front of a crowded room to speak. Repeatedly exposing yourself to this would, over time, reduce the power of the negative trigger. However, because we are discussing triggers here in the context of equestrian sport, which is a high risk sport, it's really important that any attempts you make to overcome a negative trigger are done in a very controlled and safe environment because any negative triggers you have when riding may well exist because of a genuine safety concern. That's why it is often advisable to seek help from a qualified professional to overcome a negative trigger, especially if you have completed the actions I gave you in earlier chapters and you're still struggling to overcome a negative trigger.

POSITIVE FOCUS

Before we move on and look at how you can develop your own positive triggers, it is important that you understand the type of responses that you are looking to achieve as a result of the trigger.

When I work with riders, the aim of the triggers we establish is to create positive focus on the task in hand. If you've read the chapter on positive focus already, then you'll know that positive focus is a combination of being able to sustain your focus (focal endurance) and directing your focus on to positive action (focal control), which you will develop through the strategies on positive focus, as well as beliefs, mental rehearsal, inner critic and emotions. This is why I have deliberately placed this chapter on triggers at the end of the book. Remember that to get the best from triggers, you really need these other mindset strategies in place first. Because once you have these in place, you can work out how to create triggers for positive focus.

Everyone experiences positive focus differently so it is important that you get connected with what positive focus feels like for you. Here are the most common features of positive focus that many riders experience:

- Motivated, psyched up and ready to go
- In control
- Focused
- Confident
- Time slows down
- Effortless and easy feeling
- In the zone
- Unaffected by distractions
- Quiet mind
- Breathing slowly
- Only aware of yourself, your horse and the next challenge
- Tuned in to your horse
- Able to make quick decisions and react quickly
- Remain focused on the task in hand
- If a mistake occurs, you simply move on and focus on the next movement or jump

GET TRIGGER POWER

1. Focus on what you want

The first step to trigger positive focus is to focus on what you want. Consider what you want to achieve and then reflect on how you need to ride to achieve your goal. Focus on the positive actions you can take that will help you achieve your goal. You may not be able to control the outcome but if you direct your focus so that you ride more positively and effectively under pressure, you give yourself a better chance of achieving the outcome you want.

2. Identify a trigger

Triggers are very individual and vary from rider to rider. This step is all about tapping into your own experience rather than trying to copy someone else. What works for someone else won't necessarily work for you.

Remember that a trigger is something that produces a behavioural response. It will be something you have learnt, just like Pavlov's dogs. I am a big fan of identifying quick wins, and when it comes to identifying a trigger, your quick wins are hidden in amongst your life experiences.

When I work with riders, I ask them a series of questions to understand what positive triggers they currently have in other areas of their lives outside riding that could be repurposed and used in challenging riding situations and at competitions.

Think about what makes you feel confident, in control and positive. Make a list and identify some potential triggers. If you're struggling to identify an existing positive trigger from other areas of your life that will give you positive focus, here are some examples of triggers you could use:

- Song: music can often hold powerful triggers. I have a song that I play every time I'm preparing for a speaking event because it helps me get into my performance zone. I don't play it at any other time because I want to maintain its power.

- "Lucky socks": this can be socks, another piece of clothing or any other physical item like a tie pin or a piece of riding equipment that makes you feel good. It doesn't have to make you feel lucky, it can simply make you feel powerful and in control, as if it gives you some magic super power. The important thing here is that it triggers positive focus for you so it doesn't matter if you think it's superstitious. If it has the desired effect, that's all that matters!

- Catchphrase: words have meanings and can evoke powerful emotions. Think about the words and phrases you use when you're in your zone. Perhaps it's something you say to your horse like "Get on" or "Let's do this." The best catchphrases are the ones that are stated positively. Avoid negative phrases like "Don't mess this up." Negative phrases are negative triggers. Whatever phrase makes you feel confident, focused and in control, can be used as a trigger by saying it in your head or out loud, whichever works best for you. You can say it as quietly or loudly as you need; just make sure you say it confidently and calmly.

- Focus words: this is similar to a catchphrase except focus words tend to just be single words that give you a command that helps you to refocus and reduce stress if you're anxious, nervous or tense. For example, if you tend to get tense in the warm-up, you may wish to use "Relax" as your focus word. Remember that, whatever focus word you choose, it must give you the desired response, so in the example I just gave, saying "Relax" will only be a trigger for you if it actually helps you to relax. It's best if you say your focus word out loud and remember you can say it as quietly or loudly as you need; just make sure you say it confidently and calmly.

- **Action:** sometimes just doing something can help you to regain confidence, focus and control in challenging situations. This is the type of trigger that most people associate with superstitions. In tennis, you may see players bouncing the ball a set number of times before they serve, repeating that same action in the same way every time they serve. They are using this as a trigger, a cue, to focus positively on the task in hand. As a rider, there are so many actions you have to do before you even get on your horse, that you have lots of options. Just remember that it needs to produce the exact response you want, e.g. confidence, focus, sense of control. Examples of actions that some riders have used include buttoning up their jacket or zipping up their body protector, zipping up their riding boots and putting spurs on. Reflect on the actions you use in everyday riding situations and at competitions with your horse that help you to feel confident and positively focused. Remember that most of the time you are unaware of your triggers and this exercise is all about becoming more aware of what your positive triggers are, so you can use them strategically when you ride and compete.

- **Mascot:** this is a small object that you can carry around with you. This could be anything but it needs to be small and safe enough for you to have with you when you ride. If you compete, the mascot needs to be something that is allowable within the rules set by the competition organisers or federation/governing body. The mascot needs to be something that you associate with being in control and feeling confident. The idea of a mascot is that you can touch it when you need to, when you need a confidence boost or need to refocus.

- Affirmations: these are positive phrases designed to make you feel confident and require practise to make them effective triggers. An example would be "I meet every situation knowing I am its master" or "I confidently overcome whatever challenge is in my way." If you say these phrases repeatedly every day you'll start to build stronger belief in them, and then you can use this as a trigger to help you feel confident when you need it.

To help you identify your triggers, write this sentence down and fill in the blanks for anything you think is a trigger, so you can clearly see the cause and the effect and work out if it helps you feel more confident, focused and in control:

When I see/hear/feel/experience (BLANK), I feel/do (BLANK)

3. Plan to use it

Once you have identified your triggers you then need to work out when you will use them. It is best to use triggers when you need them the most. I recommend you use the trigger just before or as you notice yourself starting to become anxious, nervous or stressed. As a rider, there are so many actions you have to complete before you get on your horse, that you have lots of options. You can also use a trigger to refocus yourself just before you enter the competition arena. You can also incorporate triggers into your pre-competition routine to help you feel prepared and focused before you arrive at the competition. It is important that you create a clear plan so that you know which triggers you will use and when to help you remain confident and focused. You will find it helpful to mentally rehearse using these triggers, and you can even incorporate this into your training sessions so you remember exactly when to use them.

ACTION

Complete steps 1 to 3 in the Get Trigger Power section of this chapter.

NOTE ON TRIGGER CREATION

This chapter has focused on using existing triggers derived from your life experience to help you ride at your best in challenging situations. If you want to create brand new triggers, be aware that this is a mechanical process that requires your brain to learn to associate something with a feeling. You'll need to establish a new connection between a stimulus and a behavioural response. This can take time and I recommend seeking help from a professional, qualified in neuro-linguistic programming (NLP) or sports psychology to get the best and most effective results as quickly as possible.

PERCEPTION IS KING

The reason I am so passionate about encouraging you to use triggers is because perception rules. Perception is reality. Whatever you believe helps you to ride at your best, will help you. It doesn't matter if other people think you are crazy or superstitious; all that matters is that it works for you. If you have time, I encourage you to Google "placebo effect" and read all about amazing studies of how our ability to believe in something allows us to overcome obstacles and achieve truly outstanding things.

Here's just one example. Whilst treating wounded American soldiers during World War II, a doctor called Henry Beecher faced a dilemma when his supply of the painkiller morphine ran out. Medical supplies were in short supply, so with no option to get any more morphine at short notice, Henry made an important decision. He decided to inject soldiers with saline solution (salt water) and told the soldiers they were being injected with morphine. An amazing 40% of the soldiers reported that the saline injection eased their pain.

This is just one example of how powerful our perception really is because it can change our reality!

That's why I encourage you to be creative and give yourself permission to believe in your triggers and ignore the cynics. Rational thinking absolutely has its place in the world and without it we wouldn't have a structured, ordered society. Belief can elevate you to a new level of performance power and, once you discover that, you won't want to go back. It will open your eyes to possibilities you didn't see before and enable you to achieve riding goals you may not have thought were possible.

FINAL THOUGHTS

How will I ever get back on...

I worked with a rider a few years ago who had suffered a number of falls from her horse and despite buying a new horse, realised that her confidence was shattered. She came to me because the thought of riding and jumping made her anxious and she wanted to learn how to control her nerves. She loved Eventing and wanted to return to competing, with the aim of progressing her young horse through the levels. She told me that her loss of confidence had been devastating and she desperately wanted help to rebuild it so she could reconnect with her love of riding and competing again. She described how debilitating her anxiety had become, to the point that she would feel frozen in the saddle. Showjumping rounds had become three minutes of crisis management rather than a round where she rode from fence to fence. She would enter the arena, her mind blank, unable to ride positively and rails fell as a result. We discussed the causes of her nerves and strategies to manage her emotions and create more positive focus. These strategies included breathing techniques, mental rehearsal, self-belief and setting clear goals. As a result of applying these strategies consistently, she was able to calm her nerves and restore her self-belief. This meant she was able to return to Eventing and progress through the levels, achieving a double clear on a number of occasions. She got in touch recently to tell me that she is still enjoying Eventing and continues to use the mindset strategies to help her remain confident and focused under pressure.

Practise and preparation are absolutely key to making lasting improvements to your mindset. The mindset strategies I've outlined in this book complement the technical preparation and practise you do with your instructor or trainer. These strategies do not replace technical preparation and practise! If you're unprepared for a challenging riding situation, whether it's at competition, in training, schooling or hacking, your emotions are likely to overwhelm you, and if this happens you will find it difficult to control them. In this situation, the fix is not a mindset strategy; it's technical practise. When you are underprepared and you get anxious it's because you know you are not prepared and therefore unlikely to succeed. If you are unsure or worried about any aspect of your technical practise or preparation before a competition, you must discuss this with your instructor. Be as specific as possible when you explain what you are experiencing so your instructor understands exactly what is happening and can help you find a solution.

So, did you take the actions I gave you in each chapter of this book? When you accurately and consistently apply the strategies in this book, I am confident you will improve your riding performance, and you may even be pleasantly surprised by the results you achieve.

This book provides you with a solid foundation of tools and techniques that will help you to build a confident and focused mindset so you can deal with pressure more effectively. If you'd like to find out more about rider psychology coaching then check our my website for further information: www.rezonecoaching.com

WISHING YOU EVERY SUCCESS ON YOUR JOURNEY TO BUILDING CONFIDENCE AND FOCUS!

Printed in Great Britain
by Amazon